PHILOSOPHY AND ARGUMENT

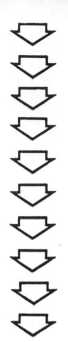

PHILOSOPHY
AND
ARGUMENT

Henry W. Johnstone, Jr.

THE PENNSYLVANIA STATE UNIVERSITY PRESS

To My Mother and Father

Contents

Acknowledgments

Undoubtedly my greatest indebtedness is to Professor J. William Miller, for my interest in pursuing the studies which resulted in this book grew out of my association with him at Williams College. However, Professor Miller should not in any way be held responsible for the outcome of this investigation, the bulk of which was carried out after the period of our association.

Professor Gilbert Ryle has commented on several versions of the manuscript, and I am particularly indebted to him for advice on style.

Others from whose written or spoken comments I have especially benefited I list in alphabetical order since it would be difficult to say which have helped me the most. These are Professors John M. Anderson, Leo J. Apostel, Lewis White Beck, and Walter Cerf; Mr. George Chatalian; Professor H. A. Finch; Dr. Robert Gahringer; Mr. John Kozy; Professors C. I. Lewis, Homer E. Mason, and Harry Nielsen; Mr. Herbert R. Otto; Professor Ch. Perelman; and Dr. James Sheridan.

For permission to reprint passages from my articles, I am grateful to the editors of the following journals:

The Journal of Philosophy ("Philosophy and *Argumentum ad Hominem*," Vol. 49, 1952, pp. 489-498; and "The Nature of Philosophical Controversy," Vol. 51, 1954, pp. 294-300)

Philosophy and Phenomenological Research ("A New Theory of Philosophical Argumentation," Vol. 15, 1954, pp. 244-252; "Hume's Arguments Concerning Causal Necessity," Vol. 16, 1956, pp. 331-340; and "Argument and Truth in Philosophy," Vol. 18, 1957, pp. 228-236)

Methodos ("The Methods of Philosophical Polemic," Vol. 5, 1953, pp. 131-140)

Dialectica ("Some Aspects of Philosophical Disagreement," Vol. 8, 1954, pp. 245-257)

Mind ("The Logical Powerfulness of Philosophical Arguments," Vol. 64, 1955, pp. 539-541)

Logique et Analyse ("Systèmes formels et systèmes ontologiques," Vol. 1, 1958, pp. 24-27)

I wish to thank the following publishers and editors for permission to quote from the works mentioned:

The Oxford University Press (Cornford's translation of Plato's *Republic,* and H. W. B. Joseph, *Logic*)

Presses Universitaires de France (Perelman and Olbrechts-Tyteca, *Rhétorique et Philosophie*)

The editor of *Revue Internationale de Philosophie* (G. Ryle, "Proofs in Philosophy," 1954)

Allen and Unwin (W. M. Urban, *Beyond Realism and Idealism*)

The Columbia University Press (Hope's translation of Aristotle's *Metaphysics*)

The Odyssey Press (Wheelwright, *Aristotle*)

The Princeton University Press (Ledger Wood, *The Analysis of Knowledge*)

The editor of *The Journal of Symbolic Logic* (John Kemeny, "Models of Logical Systems," 1948)

I wish to express my gratitude to the Council on Research of The Pennsylvania State University and to its successor, the Administrative Committee on Research, for the financial assistance they gave me during much of the time that this book was in preparation.

Finally, I am indebted to the Belgian American Educational Foundation, Inc., for the grant of a Special American Fellowship during the Spring of 1957, during which a substantial portion of this book was written.

H. W. J., Jr.

University Park, Pennsylvania

April 15, 1959

Ist die Widerlegung [eines Princips] gründlich, so ist sie aus ihm selbst genommen und entwickelt, — nicht durch entgegengesetzte Versicherungen und Einfälle von außenher bewerkstelligt.

— Hegel

I

Introduction

If two men disagree over how many l's there are in "Fulbright," or whether methyl alcohol has a higher boiling point than water, or whether there is any water vapor in the atmosphere of Venus, or whether strife in the Middle East can be prevented from igniting a world war, each can interpret the disagreement as consisting of the fact that the other has made a statement incompatible with the one he has made. Both can, without any difficulty, understand both statements in question. Convinced as either may be of the truth of his own statement, he can at least imagine what it would be like for his opponent's statement to be true. The conflicting statements are thus at least logically commensurate.

When two men disagree over fundamental philosophical issues, however, neither is quite entitled to be able to imagine what it would be like for his opponent's statement to be true, even though one or the other may be under the illusion that he can. For each, in stating his own systematic position, is in effect claiming that this position includes all the relevant evidence and therefore no statement adducing evidence against it is possible. Whoever asserts, for example, that the individual is the product of his heredity and environment is, in principle, incapable of conceiving any factors contributing to the make-up of the individual that are not reducible to heredity and environment. To attack this view by appealing to such extraneous factors is to beg the question; for it is to assume that extraneous factors are possible, which is precisely what is denied by the statement that the individual is the product of his heredity and environment. The question-begging character of the attack is confirmed by the effortless ease with which the defendant can reduce any alleged- ly extraneous factor to a factor of heredity or environment. The view is thus not logically commensurate with views that oppose it. Similarly, if one takes the position (apparently taken by the existentialists) that authentic existence is more important than technological progress, one will not be able to think of techno- logical progress as having any importance at all except to the perhaps accidental extent that it enhances authentic existence; so that it will be impossible, strictly speaking, even to imagine technological progress as more important than authentic exist- ence. This situation is entirely different from that in which a man claims that the problem of feeding the world is more im- portant than that of conquering space, for he can at least imagine what it would be like for the opposite to be true.

To a neutral observer of the issue whether the individual is the product of his heredity and environment, or of the issue whether authentic existence is more important than technological progress, the logical incompatibility of the opposed statements at issue may, of course, seem obvious. This is because such an observer need not endorse the claim of either position to include all the relevant evidence. Even the defendant of one of the posi- tions involved may, of course, at times assume the role of neutral observer. The existentialist can speculate about the relative mer- its of existentialism and pragmatism. But when he does, he is neglecting for the moment the fact that existentialism can be an actual philosophical position only when it claims that no other position is even possible.

I shall want to discuss the opposition of opposing philoso- phical positions in greater detail. I cannot do this directly until I reach Chapter VIII of this book, but in the intervening chap- ters there will be found some suggestions that amplify what I have already said about the nature of philosophical opposition. For the most part, the intervening chapters develop ramifications of the view that the opposition is not fundamentally logical. Chapter II is an exploration of some of the consequences of supposing that the opposition between conflicting philosophical positions is more radical than any purely logical opposition between statements. It has been thought that the radicalism of the opposition is the symptom of an inherent defect of human reason or the insuperable differences in the personalities of those who disagree. After reviewing such diagnoses, I shall try to show that the only proper response to disagreement as radical as that found with respect to philosophical positions is participation in genuine controversy. In Chapter III, I shall contend that not only is it impossible to cross the abyss that separates opposing philosophical positions unless the partisans of these positions are willing to argue with each other, but also argument is the sole medium through which a position can communicate its content, even if it faces no opposition. For, as I shall attempt to make clear, any philosophical statement viewed apart from its argumentative context is profoundly ambiguous.

Chapter IV attempts to deal with a problem directly raised by Chapter III. Obviously not every argument serves to clarify the meaning of a given philosophical statement or to cross a given philosophical abyss. The clarification or transit can occur only if the argument is valid in some relevant sense, even if not in the sense in which arguments that submit to the analysis of conventional logic can be valid. But such an extension of the concept of validity immediately raises the question, "How are *valid* philosophical arguments to be distinguished from *persuasive* ones?" In Chapter IV, I shall try to answer this question by maintaining that there is an obligation to accept the conclusion of a valid argument, and that whether this obligation is, in fact, associated with any given philosophical argument is altogether independent of the extent to which the argument is persuasive.

Chapters V and VI will attempt to ascertain the sense in which philosophical arguments can be valid. Here I shall try to show that while *argumentum ad hominem* is not usually regarded as sufficient to establish any conclusion (indeed, it is usually simply dismissed as invalid), there are cases in which *argumentum ad hominem* alone suffices to establish a philosophical conclusion. Furthermore, the abyss that separates conflicting philosophical systems precludes any use of *argumentum ad rem;* for to appeal to e v i d e n c e in attacking a position that claims to include all the evidence is to beg the question. Thus every valid philosophical argument is *ad hominem*.

In Chapter VII, I shall try to apply my theory of validity to Hume's arguments regarding causation and causality. I have selected these arguments as an example because they are among the most influential arguments in the history of philosophy. Any theory of philosophical argumentation that fails to do justice to them probably ought to be viewed with suspicion. The only purpose of this chapter is to test the plausibility of my theory.

Chapter VIII can be regarded as a direct discussion of the nature of philosophical opposition. Philosophical systems of a type that I shall call "ontological" are treated as a paradigm for the relations among philosophical positions in general. Here I shall also consider how the structure of an ontological system differs from that of a logical (formal) one. This chapter is somewhat more technical than the rest of the book. The general reader could omit reading it without detriment to his understanding of the material that follows it.

The final chapter is concerned with the nature of the *homo* to whom the valid philosophical *argumentum ad hominem* is addressed. I have already mentioned an obligation to accept the conclusion of a valid argument. This obligation, like any other, reveals something about the nature of the person whose obligation it is. Accordingly, I shall sketch out the view of personality — I shall actually use the word "selfhood" — that seems to me to be implied by the possibility of valid philosophical arguments.

I turn to my general line of defense against what is certainly the most serious charge likely to be made against this book: the charge that I am primarily engaged in meta-philosophy. By "meta-philosophy" is meant theory about the motives for making philosophical statements, the conditions under which philosophical problems arise, the nature of philosophical dispute, and so on. Theory of this sort is regarded as objectionable for at least two reasons. First, meta-philosophy seems to threaten the autonomy of philosophical activity. If the theory of that activity could exhibit it as wholly the expression or product of nonphilosophical activities of a more fundamental kind — of psychological, social, or economic activities, for example — the philosopher would no longer be entitled to take his own work seriously. But an essential characteristic of philosophical work is that it cannot be done at all unless it is taken seriously. The second objection against meta-philosophy is that even if it does not aim to undercut philosophical activity, or succeed in doing so, it is idle. Instead of addressing itself to the solution of philosophical problems, it merely talks about the ways in which other people have proposed to solve them. It is a parasite feeding upon living philosophy.

Yet even if this book is primarily a study in meta-philosophy — and I am not at all convinced that it is — I am not, in any event, attempting to construct a theory about philosophy that reduces it to nonphilosophical considerations. There are, of course, analyses of philosophical argumentation that propose or presuppose just this reduction. It is possible, for example, to attempt to exhibit philosophical argumentation as simply an instance of argumentation in general. This would presuppose that philosophy is continuous with discourse in general, and might be open to the objection that it reduced philosophical to nonphilosophical activity. Examples are provided by recent analysis and positivism, which have, in effect, sought to criticize the arguments of philosophers in terms of the standards for arguments in ordinary language or in science. But all this is exactly the opposite of what I am doing. What I have already said about the peculiar status of philosophical argumentation implies that I regard philosophy as *sui generis*. It appears, then, that whether what I am doing is meta-philosophy or not, my position is not open to the objection that it reduces philosophy to anything else.

Nor is it open, at least in any obvious way, to the criticism of failing to deal directly with philosophical problems. I take seriously the platitude that the nature of philosophy is itself a philosophical problem. But to say that philosophy is *sui generis* is already to say something about the nature of philosophy. It is at least implicitly the result of an effort to solve a philosophical problem. Furthermore, this is not by any means the only philosophical problem with which I deal in this book. I have already indicated that I regard certain general features of the self as fundamental to my account of philosophical argumentation. But the question of the nature of the self is nothing if not a philosophical question. I am not at all sure, moreover, that the book does not involve additional problems as well.

Over and above the defense I have just outlined, there are
one or two remarks I should like to make about meta-philosophy
and the objections to it. In the first place, I doubt that meta-
philosophy is, strictly speaking, even possible. The term usually
is used to denote an activity that criticizes philosophy from a
philosophically neutral point of view. In my opinion, however,
any point of view from which criticisms can be made must be
philosophical. It is a commonplace that even the most objective kind of criticism, including the scientific critique of experience, presupposes a philosophical point of view. I am not supposing, of course, that this commonplace justifies my opinion; it
only illustrates it. But in view of the possibility that I might be
right, there is something strange about accusing a person of doing meta-philosophy. Is he being accused of doing what no one
can possibly do? Or is he just being accused of claiming to do it,
without actually succeeding? In the latter case, what he ought
to be accused of is not doing meta-philosophy, but doing philosophy.

My second remark is that it has always been supposed that
one of the most important functions of philosophy is to elicit and
systematize the standards of judgment in all areas in which judgments occur. But philosophy itself is one of the areas in which
judgments occur. Thus one of the very motives for engaging in
philosophical activity should dictate the examination of philosophical activity. But if meta-philosophy is in any way possible,
it is difficult to see what it could be claiming to provide other
than just this examination.

My own conclusion is that it is not particularly illuminating
either to call oneself a meta-philosopher or to accuse another of
being one. There seems to be no way of drawing a tenable distinction between philosophy and the theory of philosophy. Every
philosophy asserts or presupposes a view of the nature of philosophy. Conversely, any such view — of which the content of
this book is an example — is itself philosophical.

A second main objection that may be urged against my
theory of philosophical argumentation is that the only philosophical positions I have taken into account as subject to argumentative elaboration, defense, or attack are unimportant and
atypical. Most positions, it will be said, make no claim to include

all the evidence — not because they are diffident in this respect, but because they are fundamentally attempting to make some quite different point. It would be foolish of me to attempt to anticipate the examples that could be adduced in support of this contention; any major position in philosophy might well serve as a plausible example. In saying this, I mean to be admitting the force of the objection. My only defense is that whatever point a position explicitly attempts to make, it is fruitful to think of the attempt itself as having a certain structure; and to say that the position claims to include all the evidence is one way of formulating this structure. Nor would I wish to maintain that every attempt to establish a philosophical point actually exhibits this structure. The structure and the forms of argumentation to which it gives rise are standards from which actual philosophical discourse may depart, just as ordinary discourse departs more or less widely from the standards of validity proposed by the organon of logic. The implication is that what I shall have to say about the forms of philosophical argumentation is normative rather than purely descriptive. It is in making this distinction that I am able to face the charge of having misdescribed actual philosophical positions and arguments. But of course the distinction carries with it an obligation. Whoever asserts that his analysis reveals what ought to be in independence of what actually is, assumes the obligation to show that what he thinks ought to be does have value. It is primarily the sense of this obligation that has led me to write Chapters VII and IX of this book. I have analyzed Hume's arguments in the hope of showing that to the extent that they conform to the standards I recommend they are in fact forceful, and that they lack force to the extent that they depart from my standards. My account of the self is intended to show that what conforms to these standards also has the merit of conforming to certain important demands of human nature.

II

Some Aspects of Philosophical Disagreement

It is a disconcerting experience to become aware for the first time of the existence of philosophical disagreement. The individual who sees, however dimly, that not everyone shares his fundamental beliefs senses that these beliefs, and the world projected by them, are threatened. At first, perhaps, the danger is felt to lie not in the possibility of having the wrong beliefs, but just in the identification of one's beliefs as such. An inarticulate and immediate certitude seems, as the result of articulation, to have become a little remote. What was hitherto totally indeterminate now assumes limits. The individual feels that the range of his thought is somehow circumscribed, and that he can no longer act without a certain embarrassed self-consciousness.

For a time, the individual may attempt to dismiss the threat by supposing that those whose philosophical beliefs differ from his are, after all, "not like him." They are beyond the pale; what they happen to believe need have no effect upon him. But the damage has already been done, even if the threat was only apparent; his beliefs have now come definitely into view and cannot revert to their original and innocent indeterminateness. Furthermore, he will inevitably perceive that those other people are "like him" in at least one respect that justifies his alarm. Like him, they are human, and so are committed to philosophical beliefs, for better or for worse, even though they may actually be entirely unlike him in all other ways. The reality of the threat is thus confirmed.

The threat to belief arising simply from the identification of it as belief now becomes the more powerful challenge of negation. The individual who saw his belief assuming limits was *ipso facto* aware that alternative beliefs were possible. But the recognition that there are really others whose beliefs differ from his transforms possibility into actuality and turns an abstract alternative into a concrete negation. This negation is just an explication of the presentiment of danger that generated the problem in the first place. Without it, there could be no problem and no escape from naïveté.

Relief from this negation is sought by the individual in the presumption that his own beliefs are true while those that differ from his are false. The idea of truth thus first occurs to him as a response to his problem, and not as an initial datum of the problem. But his insistence that the philosophical beliefs of certain other people are false puts him in a position which he will eventually find intolerable. That other humans should be misguided in matters of such fundamental significance will begin to impress him as an unmitigated evil in two distinct senses. A man who will not acknowledge the truth is immoral, and a universe that conceals it from him is cruel. Presently the desire is conceived to take practical steps against these defects. He who undertakes to inform others of the truth helps both men and the universe to fulfill their respective obligations.

The feasibility of this mission is, however, brought into question by the reflective individual. Is it really possible to inform others of truths of the sort now under consideration? One person informs another when the latter is ignorant of certain facts. But those whose philosophical beliefs are opposed to one's own are not merely ignorant of certain facts. Indeed, it now becomes clear that they stand morally condemned not for ignorance, but for refusing to acknowledge the truth even though in possession of all the facts; ignorance might be excused, but not stubbornness. To suppose that one can inform these others is to deny the very waywardness in them that led to one's moral concern with them.

So long as the problem remains moral, one can neither retreat nor advance: the thoughtful individual can neither tolerate what he regards as deviation from the truth nor eliminate it. He may briefly consider manipulating his antagonists through propaganda or force. It becomes at once obvious, however, that neither

of these instrumentalities is appropriate. The moral problem
arose only because it was presupposed that the others were free
to reach their own philosophical conclusions. If one treats them
as though they were not free, one is no longer entitled to pass
moral judgments upon them, and the problem that led to this
treatment is not solved but repudiated.

Without requiring any further insight, the individual now
can summarize his impasse in philosophical terms. The evil that
confronts him cannot be overcome by means of any finite technique. It is a necessary aspect of finite experience. And once
the problem is put in these terms, the first step toward its resolution becomes clear. A necessary evil ceases to be morally and
intellectually intolerable only when exhibited as a type of necessary appearance. Thus there arises the demand for a philosophical theory of disagreement.

The simplest sort of theory is that on which the apparent disagreement is viewed as being in reality purely verbal. Those
whose philosophical beliefs seem to differ may, in the first place,
be consciously dissembling when they express these beliefs in
conflicting ways. The beliefs themselves may be the same —
perhaps even entirely nonexistent and therefore vacuously iden-
tical. Thus philosophical disputation is nothing but logomachy
— a battle of mere words to which, as the disputants themselves
know, there corresponds no real difference of opinion. The un-
philosophical mind has, of course, entertained this suspicion
throughout the history of philosophical disagreement. But when
formulated as an explicit theory, the suspicion will not withstand
criticism. Intrinsically, it fails in not being able to account for
the disagreement that it must itself engender: the disagreement,
that is, between those who maintain that philosophical disagreement results from conscious dissembling and those who maintain
that it does not. Can the belief in both cases be the same? Ex-
trinsically, it also fails, for it does not supply any motive for the
behavior it imputes to disagreeing individuals. Why should people always express their beliefs in consciously misleading ways?

A second and somewhat more sophisticated theory arises in
the attempt to discover such a motive. Apparent philosophical
disagreement, it is now asserted, is really a kind of game; the
motive is to win the game. On this view, the apparently disagree-

ing parties are themselves still conscious that the differences between their beliefs are not real, but they no longer primarily aim
to dissemble. Their behavior exhibits strategy, but not necessarily
misrepresentation. This theory will be recognized as only slightly
less pervasive than the first; philosophers are among its adherents
as well as nonphilosophers.

Here a new theme has appeared — that of controversy. Controversy has not characterized any of the aspects of philosophical
disagreement hitherto considered. It was not involved in the act
of ignoring one's antagonist, nor of labeling his views as false,
nor of informing or persuading him, nor of expressing one's own
beliefs in a misleading fashion. Each of these acts is essentially
unilateral; it can be carried out by one party to the disagreement
without requiring that the other do the same. But controversy is
essentially bilateral. Since games involving strategy are also bilateral, to characterize philosophical disagreement as a game suggests its controversial quality. At the present stage, however, this
quality is merely suggested. But the theme of controversy will
become more insistent and in the end will point to a resolution
of the problem of philosophical disagreement in which all its
fundamental aspects, including the temporarily forgotten moral
dimension, are maintained.

In several respects, however, the theory that philosophical
disagreements are games is defective. One criticism of it considers the significance of defeat in a game. To be defeated here
is to have been outmaneuvered, and the player who has been outmaneuvered cannot, if he is honest, reserve for himself the right
to decide whether he has been defeated or not. A party to a
philosophical dispute, however, may admit that he was outmaneuvered but insist that he was not defeated; for the verbal ex-
changes of which he was at the losing end may have entirely
failed to force him to alter his philosophical beliefs. The implication is, of course, that there was a genuine difference of beliefs.
Plato expressed this idea by saying, "Just as in draughts the less
skilful player is finally hemmed into a corner where he cannot
make a move, so in this game where words take the place of
counters they feel that they are being cornered and reduced to
silence, but that does not really prove them in the wrong."[1]

[1] *Republic VI* 487, Cornford translation

Defeat in a game is defined by the rules. This suggests another criticism of the theory in question. A philosophical dispute, rather than being governed by fixed rules, represents the effort of each disputant to enforce his own rules. Whether a given point made in the course of arguing is legitimate or relevant depends on the respective outlooks of those engaged in the argument, and the energy of each arguer is mainly concentrated on the attempt to establish his own outlook.

The insight that each party to a philosophical dispute brings his own rules with him into the argument now generates a third theory of disagreement, on which the association between an individual and the particular rules he endorses is legitimized. Since language is an immediately obvious domain of rules, it is natural to express this theory in terms of that domain. Thus it is asserted that the apparent disagreement between two persons arises from the fact that each speaks a different language: perhaps one is employing the vocabulary and grammar of Realism, while the other exhibits the verbal behavior characteristic of Idealism. That the disagreement is only apparent can, on this theory, be shown by a process of translation revealing in the end that the philosophical beliefs of both persons are the same. The view that the disputants are consciously aware of this identity must now be surrendered; disputes arise, on the present theory, only because the parties to them think that their beliefs are really different. Otherwise, the use of different languages would be pointless.

The approach to philosophical disagreement just sketched in rough outline will be recognized as an aspect of contemporary positivism. Its merit lies in the fact that it begins to do justice, for the first time, to the systematic nature of philosophical commitment. Essentially, such a commitment is not a set of independent tenets; it is a total orientation. The idea of language is a suggestive metaphor for this orientation. But the defect of the positivistic theory is that it hypostatizes this metaphor. Disagreeing philosophers do not literally speak different languages. For to the extent that different languages are genuinely different, two persons who cannot speak each other's language cannot disagree. The Englishman who says "That is a cat" cannot, for example, be disagreeing with the German who says "Das ist ein Hund," if he does not understand this statement. A prerequisite for disagreement between two persons speaking different languages is that each must be able to translate the remarks of the other into his own language. But according to the theory in question, this is precisely the condition under which the disagreement will *cease*.

The mere failure of two individuals to understand each other is never, *per se*, an incentive for either to maintain or pursue any kind of relationship with the other. But where two philosophers disagree, this very disagreement operates as an incentive to continue the discussion. Misunderstanding and disagreement are, therefore, in principle different; and one defect of the theory under consideration is that it confuses these two ideas.

It is possible, however, to discover conditions under which the difference between misunderstanding and apparent disagreement approaches an identity, and, by asserting the universality of these conditions, to transform a confusion into a doctrine. The requisite assertion now turns out to be the proposition that apparent philosophical disagreements are occasioned not by the situation in which one disputant misunderstands another, but rather by that in which at least one disputant misunderstands the grammar of the philosophical terms he employs. Misunderstanding thus is construed as a technical ineptitude; it is no longer merely the absence of comprehension as it was taken to be on the previous theory. Therefore, it is capable of giving rise to at least the appearance of disagreement, as on the previous theory it was not. The idealist and the realist cannot even seem to disagree if each is simply speaking a language not spoken by the other. But if one of them is misusing the grammar of a language both speak, or if both are doing so, the absurdity of the solecisms committed by either disputant becomes a measure of the degree to which they will appear to be disagreeing.

The doctrine just suggested seems characteristic of a broad segment of contemporary analysis. Here the criticism of disagreements has come to be seen as normative inquiry. This insight may be counted as an indisputable gain. But corresponding to it is a serious loss: the aspect of controversy has now disappeared. Grammatical analysis is not an essentially bilateral activity. The individual who is acquainted with the rules of grammar will correct the one who is not, but this is an asymmetrical relationship, or at most a nonsymmetrical one, lacking the symmetrical property of controversy. It is important to notice that the idea of correction assumes a central position in the analytic theory of philosophical disagreement, for closer examination of this idea tends to vitiate the theory. The acknowledged expert who corrects the grammar of a person unskilled in the use of a language expects no further discussion; the act is complete. The philosopher who criticizes a colleague, however, is taken aback if there is no further discussion. He feels that he has either missed his opponent's point or incorrectly judged him to be a colleague; i.e. a person capable of defending a philosophical position. Thus philosophical criticism is essentially not an act completed at a given moment. The question "When did you finish correcting him?" makes good sense, but the question "When did you finish criticizing him?" is somewhat incoherent. In identifying criticism with correction, the theory in question does not correctly construe the grammar of "correct"; it is inadequate by its own criterion of adequacy.

The plausibility of this evaluation of the analytic theory depends directly upon the presupposition of a real difference between correction on the one hand and criticism on the other. This presupposition requires further scrutiny. Adhering for the moment to the metaphor of grammar, one may at the present juncture assert with some confidence that neither correction nor criticism could in principle be effective except in appealing to a unique system of grammatical rules. Were there several alternative systems, the discussion would be stultified; one could hope for no more than a translation from one to the other, as on the positivistic theory. The difference between correction and criticism must lie, then, in the mode of reality ascribed by each to the grammatical system in question. Correction is possible only if grammar is actual; that is, only if there exists a formalized or finitely expressible set of rules to which universal appeal may be made. Once a mistake in the use of language has been corrected, the authority of such rules precludes further discussion except, perhaps, in explanation of the manner in which the rules apply to the case at hand. If discussion does ensue upon criticism, this must mean, therefore, that the grammatical system in question is not actual, not formalized, and not finitely expressible. Such a system would operate as an ideal.

The assertion of an ideal grammar of this sort becomes the basis of a further theory of philosophical disagreement. This theory begins where the analytic theory failed; it seizes the opportunity to explain why criticism, not mere correction, occurs when individuals recognize each other as philosophical colleagues. The act of recognition, it avers, is no more than an awareness that the individual one has encountered is sensitive to the ideal rules that govern discourse; he is a sophisticate, not merely a pupil awaiting correction. "Grammar" no longer seems an appropriate word for the domain of the ideal and gives way to "Truth," "Beauty," and "Goodness." Criticism assumes the form of dialectic, the co-operative attempt to attain an articulate grasp of the ideal by finding through argumentative discussion a universe of discourse common to the philosophical statements whose apparent opposition initiated the discussion. Such criticism can never be complete, precisely because its goal is ideal.

This theory of philosophical disagreement is, of all those so far considered, perhaps the closest to the heart of *philosophia perennis*. This suggests that the motive to reduce philosophical disagreement to appearance has itself been perennial. For if dialectic does have an ideal goal, then there are no genuine differences among the beliefs of apparently disagreeing individuals; there are only differences among the ways in which individuals apprehend and endeavor to express a single truth. But, as will shortly become evident, the thesis that the disagreement is only apparent becomes extremely precarious at this point.

The theory under consideration has made at least one cardinal contribution. It has endorsed the insight that philosophical truth is ideal and so cannot be wholly articulated through any finite series of expressions. But this very insight is a mortal defect. For although this theory supposes that criticism would eventuate in philosophical vision, it fails to provide any method for criticizing the vision itself. Dialectical discussion as such involves no guarantee that the ideal universe of discourse to which it conducts its practitioners will in every case be the same; and should different ideals appear as the result of different discussions, there would be no way of distinguishing true from false short of abandoning dialectic altogether and reverting to an actual authority, such as formalized grammar or its theological equivalent.

Ultimate belief must therefore be construed as incorrigible intuition differing from one individual to another. The impossibility of maintaining that philosophical disagreements are merely apparent becomes luminously clear. A monistic view of philosophical belief has been shattered and has given rise to a radical pluralism. The question "Must philosophers disagree?" is henceforth asked in all earnestness; there is no longer any disposition to suppose that the disagreement is not real.

The personal aspect of philosophical disagreement has emerged, and this is the most important insight promoted by the intuitive theory in question. Commitment becomes a "legitimate offspring of idiosyncrasy."[2] It is legitimate in default of any criterion for discriminating among intuitions. But this default cuts both ways, of course: commitment is equally a "bastard of imagination, impregnated by experience."[3] Here is already an intimation of defect.

Involved in the intuitive theory is an expressive or emotive view of metaphysics, which declares its own alliance with an expressive view of art. Philosophy is thus regarded as a form of poetry. But this situation suggests again that the intuitive theory cannot be the final one. For it fails to do justice to the factor of negation occurring in all genuine disagreement. No one intuition as such negates another; for intuitions are by definition incorrigible and so do not enter into logical relationships with each other. Although different poets have different intuitions, they cannot, in the role of expressing intuition, disagree. If philosophers are poets, then, the question "Must philosophers disagree?" gives way to the prior problem "Can philosophers disagree?"

The effort to restore negation, and to criticize philosophical commitment while maintaining its idiosyncratic nature, results in the transformation of intuition into pure reason. The extension of reason beyond the bounds of possible experience appears to afford philosophical certitude in the sense of belief conditional upon nothing. Since such belief arises in the pursuit of knowl-

---

[2] See F. C. S. Schiller, *Must Philosophers Disagree? And Other Essays in Popular Philosophy* (London, 1934) p. 10
[3] Kant, *Prolegomena*, Introduction

edge, it expresses itself cognitively rather than merely emotively, and is capable of being contradicted. The actuality of this sort of negation arises from the fact that once possible experience has been left behind, control over the direction in which knowledge may be pursued is no longer available; and so different individuals will pursue it in different directions, as is concretely shown by the existence of fundamental antinomies. Commitments are subject to criticism precisely through the exhibition of such contradictions. At the same time, commitments arise from idiosyncrasies in the sense that between any two ways of seeking the unconditioned the choice is purely personal.

One undeniable virtue of this critical theory of philosophical disagreement is its articulation of the insight that every philosophical thesis is disputable. This was an initial datum of the problem of disagreement, for the individual's awareness of a threat was just his presentiment that none of his beliefs could be warranted as finally secure. Corresponding to this undeniable virtue, however, is a systematic failure to afford any basis for distinguishing between controversy and contentiousness. When disagreement poses a threat, that is a serious business which contrasts with the sportive or splenetic activity of disagreeing for the sake of disagreeing. Yet on the critical theory disputes of both sorts arise from precisely the same necessary defect of human thought. No account is given of the stake an individual might have in maintaining a metaphysical position. If there is such a stake, commitment must be personal in a sense not envisaged by the critical theory. Indeed, it becomes clear that on both this theory and the intuitive one that preceded it, commitment taken to be personal is, in fact, accidental to the person. It is a whim, prejudice, or dogma that any given individual is free to choose or reject, as he may choose or reject a brand of cigarettes. It is impossible that opposition to such commitment should pose a fundamental threat.

The difficulty here arises because commitment is not itself regarded as an essential element of personality. And so long as the object of philosophical commitment is taken to be merely a thesis, this difficulty will persist. For a thesis considered in terms of its content alone is accidental to any personality. To say no more than that A advocates thesis X is to leave open the strong possibility that A is the victim of a preposterous accident that left him believing in X — the accident, for example, of having been indoctrinated in a certain way, or of having been brought up in a particular environment. Of course, such an accident may well be sufficiently serious to affect a man's personality as well as the thesis he advocates. The accident of a man's early environment is a case in point. But it is necessary to distinguish between a man's personality as stamped upon him by his environment and as acquired through the mastery of his environment. Only the thesis associated with personality in the latter sense is relevant to the solution of the problem at hand, for it alone stands apart from pure accidents of fortune. There is, of course, no infallible way of making this distinction. In particular, the mere statement of a man's philosophical thesis gives no clue as to whether it is actively or passively associated with personality. There is a stronger clue, however, when a genetic account of the thesis can be given. For the claim of such an account, whether or not this claim can be justified, is to trace the thesis back to a problem — in other words, to a moment when the individual faced the necessity of mastering his environment. If commitment to a philosophical thesis is understood as resulting from the attempt to solve a problem, then, even though the thesis as such may bear no internal relationship to the personality of the individual committed to it, the fact of commitment is essential to the person.

This insight regarding the relation between commitment and personality turns out to be efficacious, because the process of working it out reveals the systematic interrelations of all the insights into philosophical disagreement hitherto encountered. In the first place, the threatened individual's original defensive impulse to dismiss those of alien persuasions as "not like him" is seen to have been justified; for if commitment is essential to personality, then different commitments will define essentially different personalities. It is true at the same time, however, that disagreeing humans are alike in being human, for it is human to be committed. In his act of commitment to some particular thesis, furthermore, the individual is being true to himself. Thus the idea of truth turns out to be philosophically appropriate to the moment in which the individual faced with the problem of disagreement spontaneously made use of it.

This idea brings in its wake precisely the moral problem that it at first appeared to generate. The individual who attempts to speak and act in such a way as to remain true to himself must come into radical conflict with others no less true to themselves but according to different beliefs. He cannot sidestep the conflict merely by withdrawing the expression of his beliefs. Such sudden silence might attend the comic downfall of a buffoon, but could not be the choice of a person of integrity. Nor can such an individual overcome the conflict by using violence to annihilate the opposition. Action of that sort would bring down a tragic fate, for one does not express one's commitment at all except in communicating it to others capable of taking issue with it. The idea of expression without an interlocutor is just as incoherent as that of commitment without expression.

The committed individual must therefore act in such a way as to maintain both the integrity of his own expression and his respect for his interlocutors. Indeed, his respect for his interlocutors and their respect for him must be interdependent; he can respect them only to the extent that they respect him, and vice versa. For as soon as any party to the discussion begins to treat any other as a mere audience, rather than as an interlocutor, the discussion is threatened. Here, then, is confirmation of the *bilateral* aspect of philosophical disagreement. This is a defining characteristic of controversy, as distinct from instruction, persuasion, correction, contentiousness, or the mere disparity of points of view. And once philosophical controversy has been so characterized, it becomes clear that it can originate only from the collision of beliefs that are *systematically* structured. For the mutual respect on which it depends is an appreciation on the part of any one interlocutor of the commitment of each of the others as a coherent whole, rather than as a set of independent tenets. Were disagreement to arise only over sets of particular tenets, it could always, in principle, be resolved by compromise. Compromise, however, is precisely what the individual striving to be true to his own problem cannot accept. If he attempts to piece together particular statements that he and his interlocutors have made, in the hope of discovering or constructing a doctrine common to all, he will see, if he reflects, that the result is entirely arbitrary, having no relation to his own

problem or to that of anyone else. It is possible, perhaps, to solve
someone else's problem by compromise, but not one's own.

The *normative* aspect of philosophical disagreement is shown
by the obligation each party to a controversy seeks to impose
upon the others to accept a certain thesis, or — what is much the
same thing — by the obligation each feels to solve his own problem. That these two obligations are indeed much the same is
suggested by the bilateral aspect of philosophical disagreement.
The *ideality* of any solution is indicated by the fact that however
many consequences one may see stemming from his way of stating the solution to a problem, his interlocutors can see additional
ones. Thus philosophical truth cannot be completely articulated
through any finite series of expressions. This is a suggestion as
to how controversy may issue in a revision of philosophical commitment in spite of the fact that such revision cannot be effected
through compromise. For every philosophical thesis is *disputable*
in the sense that it is always possible to show that the thesis is
false to the problem that generated it. The series of positions
surveyed in this chapter illustrates the process through which
philosophical commitments are revised. In this case the initial
commitment was simply the belief that there is philosophical disagreement. All of this, finally, confirms that the disagreement is
personal in nature, and that it involves a genuine plurality of commitments.

The individual faced with the threat of philosophical disagreement must therefore rise to the level of controversy. If he
fails to do this, it can be only because he has repudiated some of
the genuine aspects of disagreement. And if this is what he has
done, he has no right to say that he was faced with an initial
threat.

III

Argument and Truth in Philosophy

In philosophy there is nothing in principle more authoritative than argument. There is, for instance, no philosophical way of advocating a philosophical doctrine except to produce arguments in its favor. And when arguments are brought to bear against a doctrine, if the proponents of the doctrine wish to continue to maintain it *as* a philosophical doctrine, they have no recourse except to argue in its defense. Also, when it is shown that a philosophical doctrine rests upon a specious argument, that is sufficient to discredit whatever philosophical claim the doctrine may make, even though the critic may admit the possibility of the doctrine's being nonetheless true. Only the discovery of a better argument can restore the philosophical credit of such a doctrine.

To say that in philosophy there is nothing in principle more authoritative than argument is not necessarily to deny the possibility of grounds in philosophy no less authoritative than argument. There may, for example, be philosophical "data" or "insights" with this same degree of authority. But no statement merely reporting a datum or insight is in itself philosophical; it is rather psychological or autobiographical. A statement may be philosophical, however, when it appeals to a datum or insight in the attempt to establish a conclusion of a certain type, or to refute a proposed philosophical thesis. This appeal would constitute an argument. So even if argument is not necessarily the only basis of authority in philosophy, it is at least an authoritative feature common to all philosophical discourse.

Argument is also a common feature of scientific inquiry. It is involved not only in the process of drawing general conclusions from experimental data, but also in the very act of obtaining these data, since this act presupposes that the conditions under which any experience is to count as a datum have already been decided upon as the result of an argument. The decision, for example, to regard the masses but not the colors of bodies as data for mechanics clearly rests upon an argument of some sort.

Argument would seem, then, to be ubiquitous in both philosophy and science. I want now to ask whether it has exactly the same function in both areas of inquiry. Is there any way of distinguishing one from the other in terms of the role of argument in each?

Before I attempt to answer this question, there is one point which I must try to make clear: that nothing I shall say in this chapter is intended as an analysis of scientific knowledge or activity. I shall not be expressing or defending any part of a philosophy of science. My only purpose in making any statements at all about science is to be able to make some contrasting statements about philosophy. But the contrast is of rhetorical importance only. Even if it should turn out that what I shall have to say about science is unacceptable, I would hope that this chapter could still be judged primarily on the basis of what I shall have to say about philosophy. In particular, it may be objected that science, especially in its more theoretical aspects, actually exhibits the characteristics that I shall be ascribing to philosophy. From my point of view, however, this would only mean that science, to the extent that it exhibits these characteristics, has a philosophical ingredient.

Far from contributing to a philosophy of science, the remarks I want to make go little beyond the two platitudes that facts are facts and that whoever wants the facts should look to science. As the second platitude indicates, I shall be using the term "science" very broadly, so as to include any commonly acknowledged domain of facts. "Science," in my sense, cannot be precisely distinguished from common-sense knowledge.

I turn to the question of how to distinguish science understood in this platitudinous way from philosophy, in terms of the role of argument in each. The answer to this question emerges from the discussion in some detail of one aspect of the role of argument in science. While science must use arguments to establish both its data and its general conclusions, it is only these data and conclusions that are regarded as constituting its positive content. To think of a scientific statement as true is not to think of it as the conclusion of an argument at all, but rather as the report of a fact whose existence is independent of whatever argumentative considerations led to its discovery. In order to refine this observation somewhat, I shall stipulate that the truth of any statement is *relative to argument* when it is impossible to think of the statement as true without at the same time thinking of an argument in its favor, and it is impossible to think of it as false without at the same time thinking of an argument against it. Then what at the present juncture seems important about the role of argument in science is that the truth of a scientific statement is not relative to argument. It is perfectly possible, for example, to suppose that a statement like "The sun is 93 million miles from the earth," or "Birds are warm-blooded," or "The reaction of calcium carbide and water yields acetylene," or "There is water vapor in the atmosphere of Venus," or any other scientific statement selected at random, is true without having the remotest idea what arguments establish it or tend to do so. Indeed, not only can we think of a true scientific statement as true and think of a false scientific statement as false without at the same time thinking of any relevant arguments, but we can think of any scientific statement as possibly *either* true or false without thinking of any argument either in favor of it or against it. In other words, we can simply think of the statement, without regarding it as true or false. We can just "entertain" it. What is important here is that there are scientific propositions. Examples would be the propositions that are, or are denoted by, the statements cited above, as well as those that are, or are denoted by, the contraries of these statements (e.g., "The sun is 80 million miles from the earth.").

Against the view that the truth of scientific statements is not relative to argument, it may be objected that the statements of experimental science at any given moment are open to revision; and if and when any of them are revised, argument will naturally play a role in bringing about the revision. Is not the truth of

such statements relative to the arguments that have so far established them as well as to the nonappearance to date of arguments
capable of disestablishing them? But this is at least misleading.
A proposition is, after all, true or false regardless of whatever
arguments have been devised in favor of it or against it; this is
a part of the meaning of the term "proposition." An alternative
reply is that where there is no positive assurance that future arguments cannot be brought to bear against a scientific statement,
the latter is not regarded as true at all, but only as probable or
tentative. A *true* statement is, strictly speaking, one open to no
further revision. Scientific statements are not true at all if their
truth is relative to anything, such as argument, that is capable of
serving as the occasion of revision. If true, they are, in the sense
that the present context requires, absolutely true. If experimental
science can properly make no such statements at any stage of its
history, the conclusion is not that its truths are relative to argument, but rather that the notion of absolute truth must operate
as an ideal goal of scientific inquiry. To think of a scientific statement as true is to think of it as independent of any argument,
whether or not there actually ever have been such statements.

So far I have mainly been discussing experimental science.
For my purposes, the chief difference between this and formal
science (i.e., mathematics and logic) is that in the latter the
possibility of true statements seems more readily realizable. Accepted theorems in mathematics and logic appear unlikely ever
to require substantial revision. But this does not affect the point
I am trying to make with respect to the relation between truth
and argument in science in general. The truth of a theorem is
not relative to the argument or proof that leads to its assertion.
Once proved, a theorem becomes a part of the body of positive
mathematical or logical knowledge, and may henceforth be directly appealed to as the basis for further proofs. One may not
only think of such a theorem as true, but even know perfectly
well that it is true, without having the slightest idea what arguments lead to its establishment. The independence of the theorem from the activity of proving it is further suggested by the fact
that the same theorem may be provable in a number of different
ways. The distinction between truth and provability is, finally,
one of the fundamental presuppositions of metamathematics.

Gödel's Theorem, for instance, establishes that there are mathematical systems in which not every true statement is provable.

It is sometimes said that the truth of a theorem is relative to *assumptions*. This may be the case. But it does not mean that the truth of the theorem is relative to *argument*. To say that whether the angle-sum of a triangle is or is not 180° depends upon whether euclidean assumptions are made is not the same as to say that whether the angle-sum is or is not 180° depends upon the argument one uses. Given certain assumptions, the statement is true or false regardless of the argumentative route taken from them to it.

Philosophy differs from science precisely with respect to the relation between truth and argument. No philosophical statement, I shall maintain, can be true except relatively to an argument through which it tends to be established. Thus no philosophical statement is absolutely true. Nor does this mean, as it may in the case of the statements of experimental science, merely that no absolutely true philosophical statements exist at present. It means that absolute truth in philosophy cannot even operate as an ideal goal.

Consider some philosophical statements taken at random: "The good is the object of desire," "All men are created equal," "Every event has a cause," "The real is the rational," and "The Universe exhibits design." One important reason for supposing that the truth of such statements is relative to argument is that if no argument for or against the statement has been produced, it is impossible to decide what the statement means, and impossible therefore to think of it as true. We can assume that the statement *may* be true in one or more of its possible meanings, but we cannot think of it *as* true without envisaging at least a part of the range of possible meanings and arbitrarily selecting one of them as the actual one.

In other words, removed from all argumentative contexts, a philosophical statement is radically ambiguous and gives rise to intellectual giddiness or disorientation on the part of the reader or hearer. What shall we say, for instance, of "The good is the object of desire"? We might say that "good" has a great many meanings, in some of which the statement may be true and in some of which false — depending upon what "desire" is taken to mean. Similarly, "men," "equal," "event," "cause," and so on, are hopelessly ambiguous as they stand. Nor is the ambiguity of the terms they contain the only source of the ambiguity of the statements. For a given person, many of these terms would have relatively clear or vague subjective connotations. The words "real" and "rational" might evoke certain mental images or schemata. But even if they did, he could still experience difficulty with "The real is the rational." The problem here would be that of understanding the relevance to each other of two images or schemata that the person had never previously had occasion to associate. Ambiguity in general is possible not only with terms, but in the relations asserted to hold between or among them. One of the most notoriously ambiguous of all is the word "is."

A test of the ambiguity of philosophical statements is to consider the effect of being asked "Are all men created equal?" "Does every event have a cause?" and so on. Even many professional philosophers cannot answer such questions with aplomb when they are suddenly asked them by strangers. One stammers, at least until one can decide what the stranger might possibly mean.

It is possible for abstract statements and questions occurring in any field to produce a sense of disorientation in the reader or hearer; the phenomenon is not restricted to philosophy. But the disorientation produced by nonphilosophical statements and questions is only superficially similar to that engendered by philosophical ones. The unannounced question, "In the additive group of an integral domain, do all non-zero elements have the same order?" may seem even more disconcerting than "Are all men created equal?" or "Does every event have a cause?" Yet there are important differences. If the respondent can identify the question as scientific rather than philosophical, he may see that any sort of reply might lie beyond his technical qualifications; and accordingly he may demur. But it is not exactly because he feels technically unqualified that the respondent shrinks from answering whether all men are created equal or every event has a cause. It would be odd if anyone were more highly qualified to answer these questions than anyone else. Indeed, if anyone were technically qualified here, it would be the philosopher. But it is the philosopher especially who hesitates when such questions are asked. The difficulty is rather that the questions lack fixity of meaning. They swim into and out of focus. However else one may feel about the scientific question, on the other hand, one has confidence that its meaning is fixed by some prior series of definitions and theories. This is why it is relevant in this connection to consider the respondent's qualifications or lack of them. In identifying the question as scientific rather than philosophical, the respondent assumes that although it is "all Greek" to him, yet it is theoretically possible for someone to pursue a series of definitions and theories in such a way as to ascertain whether the question is well formed, and if so whether it is true, false, or perhaps undecidable. This claim does not apply to a philosophical question because it is the very possibility of pursuing any such series that seems dubious.

How might the ambiguity of a philosophical statement be mitigated? An obvious expedient might be to require that each statement be accompanied by a glossary of the terms occuring in it. For even if the ambiguity should turn out to reside not in the terms themselves but in their relationships, the first step toward resolving it would be to define the terms. It might be stipulated, for example, that in the statement "The Universe exhibits design," the term "Universe" is to be interpreted as meaning "the totality of possible objects of knowledge," "exhibits" as meaning "permits the possibility of discovering," and "design" as meaning "order." Now it may be supposed, at least for the moment, that "The totality of possible objects of knowledge permits the possibility of discovering order" avoids the ambiguity of the original statement. But precisely to the extent that it does, it suffers from a new defect: it is trivially true. Knowledge being, among other things, the discovery of order, the statement that the totality of possible objects of knowledge permits the possibility of the discovery of order is tautologous. Let us try again. Perhaps the meaning of "design" should be spelled out as "an all-embracing system of means to a single end." But this poses a dilemma. Does the "single end" itself belong to the Universe or not? If not, then by the definition of "Universe" it is not a possible object of knowledge, and thus could not in principle be discovered. If so, then it is one element of the Universe that does not exhibit design in the sense defined, since it is not a member of a system of means. In either case we have contradicted our-

selves. The inevitable result of attempting to interpret the original philosophical statement in such a way as to overcome its
ambiguity, then, seems to be either triviality or inconsistency.

As a further exercise of this sort, we may try to supply meanings for the ambiguous terms in "All men are created equal." We
may define "men" as "members of the species *homo sapiens*,"
"created" as "born," and "equal" as "falling within a certain range
of anatomical and physiological characteristics." But since a bio-
logical species is, by part of its definition or an immediate consequence thereof, a class of individuals falling within a certain
anatomical and physiological range, we have produced a tautology. Let us accordingly revise the definition of "equal" to read
"falling within a certain range of moral characteristics." Since
moral characteristics essentially are acquired characteristics, depending upon training and the exercise of freedom, it is self-
contradictory to assert that men are born with them. Thus "are
created" must be redefined as "possess the potentiality of." Yet
this, too, is inconsistent, because idiots are by definition members
of the species *homo sapiens* who do not possess the potentiality of
falling within any range of moral characteristics. It follows that
"men" must be given a new interpretation. But how can we interpret this word except as denoting members of the species
homo sapiens who do possess the potentiality of falling within a
certain range of moral characteristics? This yields another tautology.

Much the same series of impasses arises if we take "equal"
to refer to rights or duties instead of potentialities. The attempt
to define the ambiguous terms in both this statement and "The
Universe exhibits design" could be prolonged by exploring further corridors of the dialectical labyrinth in which each is incar-
cerated. It is also reasonable to suppose that the statements that
have not been examined here would find themselves similarly
condemned. Since the dialectic in each case is already pretty
well worked out in the literature of traditional philosophy, and
since in developing it afresh we should be taking the risk of pursuing each statement beyond the field of the present general inquiry into its specialized philosophical habitat, we must be content now to let the matter rest. The question at hand is "How
might the ambiguity of a philosophical statement be mitigated?"

This question is apparently not to be answered in terms of any proposed glossary of terms.

Before making a new assault upon this question, let me call attention to one general result of the effort to supply definitions for ambiguous terms. As a substitute for "The Universe exhibits design," I proposed at one point "The totality of possible objects of knowledge permits the possibility of discovering an all-embracing system of means to a single end." But if the difficulty with "The Universe exhibits design" was its ambiguity, the proposed substitute is in fact scarcely an improvement. Instead of the ambiguous term "Universe" we now have "totality," "possible," "object," and "knowledge," each of which oscillates within its own range of possible meanings. Is totality actual or ideal? Is possibility logical or physical? Is knowledge empirical or rational? Are its objects atomic or organic? Similar ambiguities infect the remaining terms. Nor does the difficulty here reside merely in the result of analyzing the terms. In its gross effect upon a reader or hearer, the proposed substitute is vastly more disconcerting than the original statement. "The Universe exhibits design," for all the giddiness and disorientation it originally produced, seems like semantical bedrock when compared with "The totality of possible objects, etc." The same is true of "All men are created equal" when compared with "All members of the species *homo sapiens* who possess the potentiality of falling within a certain range of moral characteristics possess that potentiality," at least in its effect upon a hearer who has not yet noticed that it is a tautology. We seem to be involved in a regress. The very effort to avoid ambiguity leads to further ambiguity of a deeper kind.

In sum, one cannot hope to understand what philosophical statements mean merely by analyzing the words that occur in them. The analysis can only lead indefinitely to the need for further and more urgent analysis. If the statements have a meaning at all, an entirely different kind of account of that meaning is necessary. The failure of an analytic account suggests the possibility of a genetic one. Perhaps the meanings of philosophical statements are to be sought in the origins of the statements. Let us test this hypothesis by attempting to reconstruct the situation that leads to the utterance of "The Universe exhibits design."

This may be a situation in which the mechanical explanation of events is regarded as authoritative. Every event is seen as determined by antecedent events. There seems no reason, furthermore, for withholding this mode of explanation from psychological events. Intentions are assimilated to efficient causes. But here some thinker may resist; he may feel that unless he can maintain the independent reality of intentions, his very claim to exist as a moral agent is threatened. He has a problem that can be resolved only by finding some relation between intention and efficient cause which preserves the reality of both. One such relation is that between a machine and its maker. The machine could not have come into being unless a maker had intended it to. But mechanical laws are sufficient to explain how its parts act upon each other. The thinker resolves his problem by saying "A machine is any system of events mechanically related to each other. The Universe is in this sense a machine. The existence of a machine, furthermore, implies the existence of a maker. Therefore, the Universe had a Maker, and exhibits this Maker's design or intention."

It goes without saying that this argument instantly raises a number of serious questions. Is it, in the first place, a sound argument, or does it rest upon equivocal or false premises? Is it correct to define a machine as any system of events mechanically related to each other? Is the Universe really such a system? Supposing that the argument is sound, does it really satisfy the arguer's need to justify his *own* claim to exist as a moral agent? These are no doubt genuine difficulties. But they are difficulties that inhere in the very meaning of "The Universe exhibits design." To understand the statement is to be aware of these difficulties. But in saying this, we have admitted that we understand the statement. Its meaning is no longer unclear.

How did we achieve this understanding? Only by becoming acquainted with the use or function of the statement. Once we have seen the statement as the conclusion of an argument that arose from a problem, we are in a position to comprehend what motive there was for making the statement, and to what extent the statement itself is adequate to satisfy that motive. But to comprehend all of these things — motive, argument, and adequacy — is to understand exactly the meaning of the statement. It is to see both its scope and its limitations.

It is perhaps a little shocking to deny that philosophical statements have meaning in the more common mode in which the meaning of a statement can be ascertained no matter from what motive it was asserted. But to ascertain meanings of that mode requires precisely the type of analysis that, in my view, cannot be successfully applied to philosophical statements. No term that has been put to a philosophical use has an analysans more familiar and comprehensible than the term itself.

Having told a story of a certain kind about "The Universe exhibits design," one should be able to tell similar stories about the other statements. In the case of "All men are created equal," it might go something like this (though it need not): A situation has arisen in which there is a tendency to suppose that man is competent to conduct his own affairs in a rational and disinterested fashion. The climate of opinion is favorable to the development of a science of man. A thinker may notice, however, that the belief in innate differences among men persists as the residue of a previous nonscientific era. He may feel that an individual's claim to an inherent social status represents no more than an endorsement of just the unreason and personal interest that are, in principle, opposed by science. Race, nationality, religion, wealth, aristocratic birth, and physical prowess are all sources of power, but none involves any inherent guarantee that the power will be used in accordance with the findings of science; indeed, each is committed to maintaining itself regardless of science. From the point of view of disinterested scientific thought, all such sources of power not only operate to distort the privileged individual's thinking but also are themselves purely accidental bases of privilege. None of them has any rational connection with the status of an individual in a society constructed on a scientific model, nor does any other attribute that is explicable as wholly the result of the individual's heredity or environment. From the point of view of science, all men are equal. That is to say, *essentially* they are equal; they differ only accidentally. If the accidental differences are those that result from heredity and environment, one must say that all men are *created* equal, even though their equality is concealed by these accidents.

In some such way as this it is possible to understand the meaning of the philosophical statement "All men are created equal." There is no other way in which it is possible, since, as I have tried to show, the statement considered apart from its origins is ambiguous, and any attempt to remove the ambiguity by defining its terms leads to further ambiguity or to triviality or inconsistency. There is from the point of view of the present inquiry no new principle involved in the story I have just told. But if one notices that, like the last one, it is at least in part an outline of the argument for the statement whose meaning it is intended to explicate, a new general conclusion can be drawn. This is that *the argument for a philosophical statement is always a part of its meaning.* Furthermore, to understand a philosophical statement is to be aware of the difficulties it poses. Some of the difficulties posed by "The Universe exhibits design" were suggested, and it is clear that similar ones must inhere in the meaning of "All men are created equal." Now a difficulty of this type may be expressed as an argument *against* the statement. Thus our present generalization has as a corollary that *the argument against a philosophical statement is always a part of its meaning.*

It is now clear why the truth of a philosophical statement is relative to argument. It is impossible to think of such a statement as either true or false without at the same time thinking of arguments for or against it, because those arguments are at least a part of the very meaning of the statement. This begins to explain the contrast between philosophical and scientific statements with respect to the role of argument. In science, argument is wholly external to statement; the statement has a meaning independent of the considerations that tend to establish or disestablish it. There are scientific propositions. But there are no philosophical propositions, because there are no statements in philosophy that have a meaning independent of the considerations that tend to establish or disestablish them. They cannot be thought of at all apart from the arguments for or against them.

Let me proceed to a possible objection against this attempt to differentiate between scientific and philosophical statements. It might be asserted that although the distinction advocated in connection with formal science between statements relative to argument and theorems relative to assumption was correct, it only shows that philosophical statements in reality belong to formal science. For both accounts given of the meanings of particular philosophical statements exhibited the statements as relative to specific assumptions: for instance, that the mechanical explanation of events is the only one possible, that man is a moral agent, that there is a science of man, and so on. It may be presumed that such assumptions would occur as well in accounts of all other statements of this sort. Whether the statement is true or not depends upon the assumptions made in each case, and not at all upon the argumentative route pursued from assumptions to statement.

In replying, I wish first to call attention to the fact that the objection puts a strain upon the meaning of the word "assumption." It is true that one of the conditions under which "The Universe exhibits design" arises is a situation in which it is supposed that the mechanical explanation of events is the only one possible. But this supposition is scarcely an assumption in the sense in which, for example, the postulate of parallels is. The mathematician is free to assume the postulate of parallels or not, depending upon his purposes. The assumption he makes represents a selection from the class of possible geometries, and this class is itself a subject of possible mathematical study. But the supposition that the mechanical explanation is the only one possible does not represent a selection from a class of possible suppositions. From the point of view of the scientist who supposes it, there is no choice between this supposition and others; there is only a choice between this supposition on the one hand and irresponsibility, superstition, or nonsense on the other. In order to be scientific at all, one must suppose (or the scientist in this historical situation supposes that he must suppose) that the mechanical explanation alone is possible. This mode of explanation is not merely a supposition; it is rather a *presupposition* of scientific thinking. The scientist is free to choose his assumptions, but he is not free to choose his presuppositions. Indeed, they are not even his presuppositions; they are the presuppositions of science. Humans assume; statements and systems of statements presuppose.

In the second place, even if the suppositions that engender a philosophical statement are assumptions, they differ from the assumptions made in any branch of formal science in being incompatible, or at least in appearing so to the propounder of the statement. Indeed, it is only because "The mechanical explanation is the only one possible" seems incompatible with "Man is a moral agent" that a statement like "The Universe exhibits design" becomes necessary. The compatibility of the assumptions made in any branch of formal science, on the other hand, is a prerequisite of the development of the branch, because otherwise genuine theorems could not be derived from them. It follows that philosophical statements are not genuine theorems. Indeed, they are not theorems at all; rather, they are assertions made in the attempt to reconcile the seemingly incompatible presuppositions that give rise to them.

A third reply is also possible. As I have already pointed out, one may distinguish between the assumptions behind any theorem of formal science and the argumentative route taken from them to it. Since different routes may with equal propriety be taken, it follows that the truth of the theorem is not relative to the argument or proof that establishes it. Now in formal science the distinction between assumptions and arguments is clear. The distinction between "axioms" and "rules of inference" is, of course, basic to metamathematics. If in philosophy the corresponding distinction is not clear, it would be at least simplistic to assert that the truth of a philosophical statement is relative to assumption but not to argument.

To develop this reply, I shall begin by observing that if the word "argument" is being used here strictly to mean "deduction of conclusions from premises," then, since the premises of a philosophical argument are regarded as incompatible, all such arguments should, in principle, be reducible to the same form: "A and not-A. Therefore, A. Therefore, A or B. But, by hypothesis, not-A. Therefore, B." In point of fact, however, no important philosophical argument has this form. In particular, an arbitrary "B" is never the conclusion. The premises that give rise to "All men are created equal" do not give rise with equal cogency to "The sea is boiling hot." Thus the word "argument" is not being used here strictly in the sense of "deduction." It would be well to attempt to find out in what sense it *is* being used.

Another common meaning of "argument" is "controversy." Nothing that I have so far said in this chapter about the arguments for philosophical statements would suggest that they are connected with controversy in any important way. There is, nevertheless, a connection, and one that it is instructive to consider. Try to think of examples of allegedly philosophical arguments that involve no element of controversy. Such examples occasionally reach professional philosophers in the mail. They take the form of documents with titles like "My Theory of the Universe" submitted for criticism, or simply for endorsement, by persons with more enthusiasm for philosophy than training in it. The statements made in such documents are often supported by elaborate arguments which sometimes are original. Yet the statements usually seem eccentric. They cannot be taken seriously. What is especially troublesome in such cases is the question of what to say to the author. One cannot simply write, "Dear Sir: You are incompetent," for this is merely an evasion. One is tempted rather to ask the author just how he happened to get interested in defending such a perverse position. The presumption here is that if the man's interest could be justified, the position itself would appear less perverse. But to justify a person's interest in a position is, among other things, to draw the position into a system of relationships with other positions. It is to point out what aspects of alien positions the person wishes to deny, and what insights he aims to assimilate. It is, in other words, to place his position in a context of controversy. Only to the extent that this treatment is possible can the problems met by the position be regarded as important. A philosophical problem is important only when it represents incoherence, conflict, tension, defect, or challenge within an actual philosophical milieu; for example, the milieux that give rise to "The Universe exhibits design" and "All men are created equal." Otherwise it is merely an obsession, and the statement or system of statements aiming to meet it is an eccentricity.

Philosophical statements, then, ring true only to the extent that the arguments supporting or assailing them reflect actual clash or controversy. Argument may reflect controversy either as a virtual image or as a real one. The image is virtual when the argument arises simply as the nonpartisan effort to reconcile the conflicting presuppositions of a philosophical problem, for here controversy may itself be no more than implicit. It is real when the argument represents the partisan advocacy of one of the sides of a controversy. If there were any philosophical arguments that reflected controversy in a purely virtual manner, it would be sophistical to say that such arguments were importantly connected with controversy, for in this case one could analyze the argument as such without referring to the controversy that engendered it. But in point of fact, the arguments supporting and assailing those philosophical statements that would not be rejected as eccentric are always partisan. For the problems that these statements aim to resolve are more than merely implicit controversies; they are themselves positions adopted in controversy. Not only is the problem of efficient cause versus psychological intention, for instance, already a subject of heated discussion when the statement "The Universe exhibits design" enters the scene, but also once this statement has entered, it does not stand aloof from the discussion; it becomes itself a further side of the controversy. What I am trying to bring out here is that the relation a philosophical problem bears to any statement that is offered as its resolution is never completely expressed simply by saying that the statement is offered as a resolution of the problem. For in claiming to do away with the latter, the former *opposes* it. Both the proponents of universal mechanism and those favoring the view that man is a moral agent are likely to take issue with "The Universe exhibits design"; this is part of what I had in mind when I raised the question of the "inadequacy" of that statement in connection with the attempt to show that its inadequacy was inherent in its very meaning. The directly related assertion that the argument against a statement is part of its meaning will be recalled. Such an argument expresses the opposition between the statement and the problem it claims to resolve. The opposition between problem and statement is an extension of the initial problem or controversy. It follows that the argument for the statement is partisan, whether or not the arguer intends it to be. That the arguer's intentions have nothing to do with the matter becomes clear when we reflect that the most innocent statements are sometimes, in fact, violently controversial.

The reason philosophical argument must have a controversial aspect, then, is that unless this aspect is manifest, it is not clear that any important problem has occasioned the argument, as a result of which the statement supported by the argument appears eccentric. On the other hand, philosophical argument is defective if it is purely controversial, because in this case again the problem that engenders it cannot be accredited. Argument that aims to controvert statements without suggesting what position it intends to support or establish ranges from verbal wrangling and logic-chopping to analysis that claims to be both serious and disinterested. But it is precisely when such argument succeeds in being disinterested that it is most difficult to take it seriously. Until the reader can at least guess what point of view the writer supports, he will think that the writer's bark is worse than his bite. The bite is ineffectual because it is occasioned by no real hunger or anger. But philosophical polemic is genuinely menacing only when it manifests the polemicist's anger at what he regards as heresy or nonsense, or his hunger for the truth. Unless one can see what stake the would-be refuter has in refuting, one cannot take the refutation seriously. The meaning of "stake" here is just "problem"; unless the argument reflects a problem, it carries no philosophical weight.

Thus philosophical argument must have a domestic phase as well as an external one. It must elaborate a position in its own right and indicate the interest a philosopher has in maintaining it. While it must be partly controversial, it cannot be purely so. Indeed, the noncontroversial aspect is a necessary condition for genuine controversy. Controversy does not necessarily arise from the mere mutual confrontation of two incompatible philosophical statements. For each party can dismiss the disagreement by saying "I believe p and he believes not-p. He is, of course, out of his mind." This situation can in general be averted only if each philosopher is able to give his reasons for taking the position he does, and in such terms as will bring intellectual pressure to bear upon the other. Controversy does not arise as the result of any contradiction definable in a logic external to the two conflicting statements, but is rather a function of the inner logic of each: that is, the argument supporting each.

This much may suffice to suggest the sense, or some of the senses, in which the word "argument" is being used here, and so to overcome the objection that argument has the same function in philosophy as it does in formal science. The only similarity is a somewhat trivial one: in both cases, argument is what conducts a thinker from a set of premises or suppositions to a conclusion. But the premises in the one case are innocuous, while in the other they constitute a problem. Also, in the case of formal science they are sharply distinguishable from the argument, while in that of philosophy they are not, since the argument, by virtue of its controversial aspect, contributes itself to the problem. This shows that even if the truth of a philosophical statement were relative to assumptions (or rather presuppositions), it would also have to be relative to argument.

It is time to deal directly, rather than inferentially, with the apodosis of this last assertion. Does it ever really make sense to say that a philosophical statement is true or false? The traditional view of truth involves the assumption that only propositions are true or false. But philosophical statements are not propositions. If they are true or false, they are so in a heterodox sense in which a statement might be true or false without being a proposition. That there might be such a sense is suggested by a phrase I used earlier. A philosophical statement may "ring true." This is a figure of speech borrowed from discourse about coins. When a coin rings true, there is some probability that it is a true coin. But a true coin is not a true or false proposition. Similarly, perhaps, when a philosophical statement rings true, there is an initial probability that it is a true statement, even though not a proposition. But what does "true" mean in this context? The true coin is one that answers to certain physical and legal prescriptions for coinage. These define what a coin ought to be. To say that a coin is true is to say that it is what it ought to be. To what prescriptions, then, does a true philosophical statement answer?

What I want to maintain is that a philosophical statement is true if and only if it is what it ought to be, where "what it ought to be" is defined by the problem from which it has arisen. This thesis can be expressed more tersely by saying simply that a philosophical statement might be *true to* its problem. This abbreviation is felicitous in that it suggests a contrast between philosophical statements and propositions; the latter are true *of* something, not true *to* it. It is clear that no statement could be true *of* whatever defines what it ought to be. "All men are created equal" might be true *to* the problem from which it arises, but could not be true *of* it.

When a philosophical statement is true to a problem, it is the conclusion of an argument to which the problem has given rise. Under these circumstances, a different argument might have established either the statement in question as false or a contrary of the statement as true. Thus two contrary statements might both be true to the same problem. A statement might be true in one way and false in another. This seems to do violence to the notion of truth. Has the discussion to this point turned out to be a *reductio ad absurdum?*

I shall try to grasp the nettle. A philosophical problem is the point of origin from which a number of different arguments radiate. Each radius is terminated by a statement. Different terminal statements may be incompatible. But each refers to an original problem. It claims to be a true attempt to solve the problem, to be true *to* its problem. This claim is articulated by the argument for the statement. But there will be arguments that dispute the claim. According to them, the statement in question is false to the problem. There is no philosophical statement whose claim to be true to its problem passes unchallenged. Truth to a problem is therefore an ideal goal — a nisus of philosophical thinking that corresponds to the ideal of absolute truth in experimental science. One essential function of this nisus is to define the conditions under which it is possible to regard two philosophical statements as incompatible; namely, when both represent the attempt to solve the same problem. Otherwise, they bear no simple relation at all to each other. Unless truth to a problem were a goal, it would be impossible to identify the contrary of a statement and therefore impossible to appeal to this contrary in the effort to exhibit the statement as false to its problem.

While truth to a problem is an ideal goal, truth relative to argument is not; it is directly constituted by the argument for a statement, provided the latter actually supports the statement. It will no doubt be objected that I have failed to distinguish between the truth of a statement and the argumentative claim that it is true. But in the case of philosophical statements, there simply is no such distinction. The argument is a part of the meaning of the statement. We cannot put the argument for the statement on one side and its truth on the other, for that would imply the possibility of understanding the statement without understanding the considerations that lead to its assertion, and this possibility has already been rejected.

What has just been said would apply, *mutatis mutandis*, to a philosophical statement whose falsity is relative to argument. And since there are arguments both in favor of and against any such statement, it follows that philosophical statements are all both true and false relatively to argument. This apparent flouting of the Law of Contradiction may seem the reaffirmation of a familiar bit of metaphysical nonsense. The Law of Contradiction, however, applies to propositions only, and philosophical statements are not propositions. Furthermore, even if philosophical statements were propositions, the difficulty in question would not arise. "A proposition cannot be both true and false in the same respect." But arguments are clearly respects of philosophical statements; a statement is true with respect to one argument and false with respect to another just as, for example, a proposition is true with respect to one date and place and false with respect to others.

A related objection is to the effect that what my account really shows is that since not all of the arguments originating from a given problem yield compatible conclusions, not all can be valid. I shall have more to say later on the subject of the validity of philosophical arguments. For the moment it is perhaps sufficient to note that the arguments must yield incompatible conclusions, since they are themselves constituents of the original problem. In other words, it is a mistake to think of the account in geometrical terms. The origin is not really a point; it is rather an amorphous area not clearly distinguishable from the radii. Not even the periphery can be clearly discerned; for, after all, the argument for a philosophical statement is at least a part of its meaning.

The truth of a philosophical statement is a very much more complicated matter than is the truth of a proposition. Perhaps it is so complicated that one should drop the idea altogether, and say that only propositions admit of truth or falsehood. This alternative seems acceptable, and might even serve to emphasize the difference between the statements of philosophy and those of science. But a useful purpose, on the other hand, is served by retaining the notion of philosophical truth. It is tempting to suppose that philosophical statements, not being propositions, are at best expressions of the moods of an individual or of society — utterances of a sort that might be exhaustively investigated by psychology or sociology. That they are not, however, is implied by the fact that the possibility of both psychology and sociology rests upon the solution of philosophical problems concerning the categories into which psychological and sociological questions fall. These are, therefore, real problems. A host of other problems that evoke philosophical statements are no less real. But reality and truth are correlative. It is in order to remind ourselves of the reality of such problems that it is useful to consider philosophical statements as capable of being true or false.

IV

Persuasion and Validity in Philosophy

Although it is my view that philosophical statements are never true or false except relatively to argument, I certainly have no wish to maintain that all arguments intended to support or attack such statements succeed in doing so. Many are obviously irrelevant, inconclusive, or question-begging, and these clearly have nothing to do with the truth or falsity of the statements that they are alleged to support. If the examples of philosophical arguments that I have given have any appearance of success, it is only because I chose them with an eye to this appearance.

At this point, however, the question arises whether the appearance of success could ever be more than a mere appearance. Can a philosophical argument actually succeed in supporting or attacking a philosophical statement? Is it possible, in other words, for such an argument to be valid? The difficulty is that I have maintained that no philosophical statement is true or false except relatively to argument. One consequence is that a given statement might be true relatively to one argument and false relatively to another. It may seem obvious that in this situation not both arguments could be valid. Indeed, since I have been strongly suggesting that there is, in principle, no reason for preferring one argument to the other, it is tempting to conclude that from the point of view I am defending, both are invalid.

This temptation is reinforced by the assertion, on which in recent times many otherwise entirely divergent discussions have converged, that philosophical statements, at least of certain types, are "noncognitive." From this, it is concluded that there can be no valid arguments supporting such statements. It is not at all clear to me what it means to call a statement "noncognitive." But I think I can show that whatever it does mean, within certain very broad limits, the conclusion that there can be no valid arguments supporting philosophical statements that are noncognitive does not in the least follow. If "never true or false except relatively to argument" is one possible meaning of "noncognitive," then what I shall have to say will constitute a defense of the thesis that a philosophical argument can be valid even though its conclusion is never true or false except relatively to argument. But even if "noncognitive" does not include "never true or false except relatively to argument," it will be obvious that precisely the same considerations can be used as a defense of the thesis in question. In other words, whether or not philosophical conclusions are properly classifiable as noncognitive, these conclusions can at least sometimes be supported by valid arguments. I have chosen to conduct this discussion in terms of the adjective "noncognitive" rather than "true or false relatively to argument" primarily because in this way I make some contact with a contemporary issue, rather than confining myself to an exegesis of my own position. Since my analysis does not depend upon any precise definition of "cognitive" and "noncognitive," I shall deliberately refrain, as much as possible, from giving examples, seeing that whether a given statement is regarded as cognitive or not often depends upon such a definition.

It is certainly not obvious, to begin with, that valid argumentation could yield a noncognitive conclusion. Of course, a formally valid argument with at least one noncognitive premise could have a noncognitive conclusion; this is shown, for example, by recent work on the Logic of Imperatives.[1] But this observation is not to the point. Those who deny that noncognitive philosophical statements can be the conclusions of valid arguments are not thinking of validity in a purely formal sense. What they have in mind is rather the notion of a valid argument as one leading

---

[1] See R. M. Hare, *The Language of Morals* (Oxford, 1952)

to a necessary conclusion — a conclusion, in other words, which, in view of the argument, it is obligatory to accept. Now the existence of an obligation to accept a statement seems to create a presumption that what the statement expresses is an item of knowledge. There has been a strong tendency to suppose that the conclusion of any argument valid in this sense must be cognitive, from which it would follow that no noncognitive statement could be the conclusion of a valid argument.

But the contention that all the arguments employed by philosophers to reach noncognitive conclusions are invalid seems to require some further explanation. Is it through sheer naïveté that the philosopher uses invalid arguments? While this interpretation may hold in certain cases, it fails to do justice to the fact that some philosophers obviously capable of distinguishing valid from invalid arguments have argued for conclusions that would surely be noncognitive if any philosophical statements are. Leibniz, for example, who stated that "All is for the best in this best of possible worlds," was one of the keenest logicians of all times. Perhaps, then, the philosopher uses invalid arguments for the same reason that the scientist does; namely, because philosophical arguments to noncognitive conclusions are inductive, and no inductive argument could be, strictly speaking, valid. A moment's reflection, however, serves to show that the arguments in question are not inductive. For inductive arguments must surely have cognitive conclusions, whether "cognitive" be taken to mean "not relative to argument" or anything else that it has generally been taken to mean. There is finally the possibility that the philosopher deliberately uses invalid arguments in the effort to persuade — that his ulterior motives for seeing to it that certain noncognitive philosophical statements are accepted are sufficiently strong, in other words, to drive him to provide rationalizations for these statements, genuine reasons being unavailable. This explanation is itself persuasive, and needs to be reviewed with considerable care.

The view that the philosopher who argues to a noncognitive conclusion is aiming to persuade his audience to accept it, even though he may know perfectly well that the argument is invalid, might seem to raise questions about the candor of such a philosopher. Yet if there are no valid arguments to noncognitive con-

clusions, he is surely not attempting to do dishonestly what other
people are capable of doing honestly. In resorting to persuasion,
furthermore, he may be performing a function vital to the maintenance of society, since it is not valid but persuasive arguments,
whether valid or not, that evoke action. The choice that faces
the philosopher is not between valid and invalid argumentation,
but between argumentation that serves a social purpose and argumentation that does not. Under these circumstances, it is altogether unrealistic to accuse the philosopher of failing to be
candid.

One may be tempted to dismiss this view by simply saying
that not all philosophical arguments leading to noncognitive conclusions are intended to evoke action. But this reply might well
invite the retort that the philosopher who is not concerned with
action is not attending to his proper business. It is perhaps better
to answer in terms of a closer examination of the actual properties of philosophical arguments in general, in the hope that this
will serve not only to distinguish the use of such arguments from
the use of arguments intended to persuade, but also to contribute
to a positive account of validity in the case of the former.

I shall begin by remarking that it is commonly supposed that
anyone who makes a philosophical statement is under some obligation to respond to the criticisms of those to whom the statement
is addressed. The philosopher unwilling to discuss his own explicit philosophical statements with others inevitably invites questions regarding his right to be considered a philosopher. He need
not, of course, reply to all criticisms or questions. But associated
with any philosophical statement is a class of criticisms and questions more or less relevant to the statement, and with these he
must deal.

The obligation that I am pointing to here is no more than
an aspect of the disorientation produced by a philosophical statement or question uttered out of any argumentative context. What
appears to an observer as the phenomenological incompleteness
of such a statement appears both to its propounder and to its
critics as an ethical incompleteness — as a promise that he must
now attempt to fulfill. The discussion to which this promise commits him has, within his point of view, the same function as the
genetic story that the observer wants to be told: both are re-

quired in order to mitigate what is essentially the same incompleteness. The argument for a philosophical statement in the sense of the attempt to support it is to the argument in the sense of the résumé of events leading up to the statement as inner is to outer.

The situation described so far, however, might not appear to differ essentially from the conditions that give rise to argumentation primarily intended to persuade. The man who wishes to persuade usually cannot hope to do so merely by making a statement. He, too, must fulfill whatever promise is implicit in his having made the statement. Unless he is regarded as a prophet, he must be willing to discuss it with others and defend it against their objections. Not every objection will be relevant, but there will be a class of possible relevant objections.

It is important to notice, however, that in discussing his position, the philosopher is not satisfying a requirement of exactly the same sort as the requirement that is satisfied when the man who intends to persuade is willing to discuss what he has to say. The latter must support his views because if he does not, he is not likely to be very effective in persuading, owing to the fact that statements ordinarily have less persuasive impact in isolation than they do in an argumentative context. In addition, his audience may be disappointed by his failure to keep the promise that his utterance seemed to imply. The philosopher, on the other hand, must discuss *his* position, not in order to achieve effectiveness, but simply because he has accepted the obligation to undertake the discussion promised by his initial statement, regardless of the consequences of this discussion.

But even if the persuasive speaker — I use the word "speaker" as an obvious abbreviation for "speaker or writer" — were obligated to discuss his assertions for the same reasons that account for the philosopher's obligation, there would remain essential differences between the persuasive speaker's *method* of discussion and the philosopher's method. The aim of the merely persuasive speaker is to secure adherence to his point of view. This aim is difficult to achieve in the measure that his audience is aware that he is trying to achieve it. To the extent that the rhetorical techniques used by a speaker are recognized by his audience, that audience is alienated or left unmoved rather than

persuaded. There are no doubt many individuals who enjoy sur-
rendering themselves to a powerful speaker. But once the technical sources of the speaker's power become evident, this sur-
render loses its enchantment. Such sources of power are, of
course, capable of being appreciated as techniques. But to ap-
preciate the artistry of a rhetorical technique and to be persuaded
by that technique are two different things. The point is not merely that people want, or think that they want, to be told the truth
rather than to be managed. As a psychological generalization,
this observation is in fact open to serious doubts. The point is
rather that it is impossible to be persuaded by a technical device
at the same time that one sees it as merely a device. This is true
even if on occasion a persuasive speaker may explicitly avow his
intention to persuade his audience, and even call the attention of
the latter to the rhetorical devices that he uses. For such a per-
formance could itself be an effective technique of persuasion, provided that it were not recognized as a technique. Rhetoric is
perfect only when it perfectly conceals its own use. To be as-
sured of effectiveness, a speaker must operate unilaterally upon
his audience, and at the same time prevent it from seeing that
he is operating unilaterally.

None of these considerations, however, would seem to affect
the way in which the philosopher must conduct the defense or
clarification of his position. No philosopher worthy of the name
would wish to secure assent to his position through techniques
concealed from his audience. One reason for this is that it would
be impossible for him to evaluate such assent philosophically.
Did his interlocutor really understand his position or not? In the
situation in which the use of rhetoric is in order, this question is,
of course, pointless; so long as the interlocutor *acts* in the required
fashion, the rhetorical argument has been effective. But it is
philosophically important to know whether one's interlocutor did
understand one's position or not, if only because the problem of
comparing the implicit content of two explicitly similar avowals
is always relevant to a philosophical discussion.

It is not only for this reason that the philosopher attempts to
avoid the use of unilateral techniques of argumentation. Another
reason is that he wishes to test his assertions against the criticism
of his colleagues. He naturally wants his point of view to pre-

vail. But no philosophical purpose is served when a point of view prevails only because its author has silenced criticism of it through the use of techniques that are effective because they are concealed from the critics.

It is perhaps tempting to suppose that the whole point might be put much more briefly by simply saying that the philosopher is obligated to tell the truth. Yet while this is perhaps suggestive of the distinction I am trying to draw between the philosopher and the persuasive speaker, it is not sufficient. For the latter may intend to do no more than to carry out the obligation to tell the truth. But the kind of truth that he wishes to tell requires him to consider various ways of telling it, some more persuasive than others. The kind of truth the philosopher wishes to tell, on the other hand, is rendered less rather than more acceptable when persuasive ways of telling it are deliberately chosen. It is acceptable only to the extent that telling it is tantamount to putting it to the test critically.

The philosopher's method of discussion is thus one that avoids the use of unilateral techniques. It is, in fact, essentially a bilateral method, in the sense that the philosopher is obligated not only not to conceal from his audience any of the techniques he uses in arguing, but also to make available to it all the techniques that he does use. For if he is unwilling to submit to the very arguments he uses against others, he thereby shows that it is not criticism but persuasion that interests him. In itself, of course, this consideration is not sufficient to distinguish philosophical from rhetorical argumentation. For a unilateral appeal to emotions, to authority, to laughter, or to force does not become a philosophical discussion merely as the result of becoming bilateral, as, for example, when A, who has been ridiculed by B, ridicules B in return. Such a discussion is at best an alternation of assaults which each participant would like the exclusive right to indulge in, because he sees that his own advantage is diminished by his opponent's use of the same technique. The philosopher, on the other hand, sees that there is an advantage in the adoption of his techniques by others, because that adoption constitutes an authorization of his use of them. Conversely, each new mode of criticism to which he is willing to submit increases the arsenal of criticisms that he can in turn make use of.

Having drawn a number of distinctions between philosophical arguments and arguments intended to persuade, I want to return to the topic of validity. Let us recall that those who deny that a philosophical argument can be valid if its conclusion is noncognitive are not denying that such an argument could be *formally* valid. What they are denying is rather that it could ever be obligatory to accept the conclusion of such an argument, in view of the argument. Now I have already tried to show that the philosopher is obligated to discuss his views. But the obligation to discuss could scarcely exist unless the philosopher were also obligated to accept the *results* of the discussion. One cannot at one and the same time suppose both that the parties to a discussion are obligated to be parties thereto, and that they are also free at any time to ignore what has been said during the course of the discusion. From this I conclude that it can be obligatory for someone to accept the conclusion of a philosophical argument, in view of the argument; and thus not only that a valid philosophical argument is possible, but also that this possibility exists whether the conclusion of such an argument is regarded as cognitive or noncognitive.

Although it is my view that the philosopher is under a general obligation to embark upon discussion, I do not wish to suggest that there are any specific conclusions that he is obligated to accept. Any discussion that he pursues will surely depend, at least partly, upon the point of view that he is defending, and upon his interlocutors' criticisms of it. The obligation to accept one conclusion rather than another will arise from the discussion itself.

There may still be something puzzling about the idea of a valid argument to a noncognitive conclusion. When an argument establishes the obligation to accept its conclusion, how can that conclusion fail to be cognitive? But the notion of a valid argument as one leading to a conclusion which, in view of the argument, it is obligatory to accept does not specify whether the obligation to accept the latter is imposed on everyone or just on certain individuals. If the obligation is imposed on everyone, the conclusion is clearly cognitive, which is equivalent to saying that if the conclusion is noncognitive, the obligation is not imposed on everyone.[2] In particular, if, as I have attempted to show on independent grounds, all philosophical conclusions are noncognitive, then not everyone can be obligated to accept any such conclusion. Whenever a philosophical argument is valid, some individuals, but not all, are obligated to accept its conclusion.

If there is any residual difficulty, it lies in the idea of a conclusion that some, but not all, are obligated to accept. But there should be no mystery about this. Few indeed are the obligations that are imposed on everyone. Most obligations arise from commitments made by specific individuals, or by groups of them, and are not imposed upon those who have not made the relevant commitments. A promise is a common example of such a commitment. If in uttering a philosophical statement an individual has implicitly made a promise, then he, but not necessarily everyone, is obligated to keep that promise. He will find that as a result of his initial commitment, he must accept conclusions that not everyone need accept.

Although I have already said that the possibility of defining "noncognitive" in several different ways makes me reluctant to attempt to illustrate the points I am discussing in this chapter, I suppose I have reached a juncture at which it might be more misleading not to give an example than to give one. A familiar example — one of a great many that might equally well have been chosen — is the discussion between Socrates and Thrasymachus in Plato's *Republic*. Having asserted that justice is the interest of the stronger, Thrasymachus asks why his audience does not praise him. Now such applause might indeed have been appropriate if this assertion had been regarded as the utterance of a somewhat prophetic orator. But it is not so regarded, at least by Socrates. Before praising Thrasymachus, he must first understand him. The questions he begins forthwith to raise serve to remind Thrasymachus that he must now fulfill the obligation of clarify-

---

[2] The converse of this statement is sometimes assumed; to wit, "If not everyone is obligated to accept a certain conclusion, the latter must be noncognitive." Thus examples putatively showing that the obligation to accept certain statements (e.g., "Killing is wrong.") is effective only for certain cultures or at certain periods of history may be adduced in the effort to show that such statements are noncognitive. This reasoning, however, seems inconclusive because there are many cognitive statements that no one is obligated to accept; namely, those whose truth has not yet been established.

ing and defending his assertion. Nor is Thrasymachus unwilling to be reminded. Once Socrates' queries begin, Thrasymachus is no longer an orator seeking praise but a philosopher trying to keep a promise. There are times when he attempts to revert to a rhetorical role — accusing Socrates, for instance, of being a slanderer. But further references to his obligation to maintain his end of the discussion are sufficient to force him back to a philosophical level. Having undertaken the discussion, he has no right to abandon it. He must, furthermore, accept the results of the discussion, including, for example, the distinction between the strict and the popular sense of the word "ruler." Also, the obligation to accept this conclusion and certain others is imposed not on everyone, but on Thrasymachus and perhaps on some others who take a position similar to his. It is not, for example, imposed on those who participate in discussions in which it would be entirely pointless to introduce this distinction. Nor is it imposed on anyone who departs from the premise or assumption that it makes no sense to talk about the ideal practitioner of an art, as opposed to the actual practitioner. Socrates and Thrasymachus, on the other hand, hold in common the view that this kind of talk does make sense, and since it is a kind of talk directly related to the thesis that justice is the interest of the stronger, the distinction in question is far from pointless for them. This may be put positively by saying that they are under an obligation to consider the distinction, thus that the argument through which they are led to it is valid. But the question whether this argument is *formally* valid simply does not arise. The point that Thrasymachus, having asserted that justice is the interest of the stronger must, in view of his assumption that it makes sense to talk about the ideal practitioner of an art, go on to distinguish between the strict and the popular sense of the word "ruler" (an obligation surely not imposed on everyone) has nothing to do with the *form* of the argument here employed. To analyze this form would be beside the point.

One other idea that receives especially solid exemplification in the same passage is that philosophical discussions are bilateral. It is only because Socrates has compared the ruler to a shepherd that Thrasymachus is entitled to do so. Thrasymachus leaves no doubt that he is gratified by this unexpected authorization to use what he considers to be a devastating analogy.

The view that a valid philosophical argument obligates some individuals, but not all, to accept its conclusion serves as a reminder of the existence of genuine philosophical disagreement. It implies that any philosophical statement must be a source of disagreement between those obligated to accept it and those not so obligated. Such disagreement is radical, in the sense that it cannot be overcome through compromise. When two or more arguments lead to incompatible conclusions, compromise can be achieved only by correcting at least some of the arguments in such a way as to remove the incompatibility. But when all the arguments in question are valid, they are not subject to correction at all, so that no compromise is forthcoming.

The character of philosophical disagreement is further suggested by some remarks regarding the role of disagreement in rhetoric. Persuasive argumentation is pointless unless there is an initial disagreement that it aims to overcome. But it is impossible unless it can make use of beliefs, attitudes, prejudices, or explicit premises adopted by its audience. These constitute an initial area of agreement, in the sense that if the speaker appeals to them, the audience will not protest. There is no reason, however, why the speaker himself need espouse such beliefs, attitudes, prejudices, or premises; it is sufficient for him to be able to rely on his audience's espousal of them. Regardless of whether the speaker shares the preconceptions of his audience, and regardless of whether he actually believes in the conclusion he is attempting to promote, it is always possible, in principle, to regard him as uncommitted; for the actual commitments of the speaker do not enter into the analysis of his rhetorical success. (Of course, if his audience thinks that his actual commitments are incompatible with the conclusion he is advocating, his success will be diminished; but we can still analyze this situation without referring to the speaker's actual commitments as such.) From the point of view of the analysis of persuasion, the role of the speaker is to treat his audience as an object. He must begin by assessing as accurately as possible the initial area of agreement. He must then consider how best to exploit this preliminary situation in order to persuade his audience to accept the statements he wants it to accept — statements with which it is not yet in agreement. His task is to manipulate his audience so as to secure agreement. All relevant disagreements must be overcome. Furthermore, the attempt to overcome disagreement must itself be concealed. For the audience will wish to reserve the right to disagree with the speaker and is likely to react in an adverse fashion if it feels that he is ignoring this right. This phenomenon is probably closely related to the impossibility of persuading through a technique that is seen as a mere technique.

The wish of an audience to reserve the right to disagree with the speaker addressing it may be viewed as a desire on its part to come to its own conclusions. It is just such spontaneity, however, that the speaker must suppress, or at least restrict, if he is to perform his role of manipulating his audience. Yet he must always create the illusion that he is inviting the latter to come to its own conclusions; for if he does not, it will exercise a residual spontaneity of judgment, lying inevitably beyond his control, to reach the conclusion that its right to reach its own conclusions is being threatened. One may think of this reaction as a process through which an audience in turn comes to regard the speaker addressing it as an object whose harmful properties are well known but can be rendered ineffective by means of equally well-known precautions. This seems an appropriate fate for the speaker who has too bluntly attempted to deal with his audience as an object.

In the rhetorical situation, then, disagreement exists only to be overcome through the exploitation of an initial agreement, and the desire of an audience to reach its own conclusions must be circumvented. In philosophical discussions, on the other hand, whether there is an initial agreement or not, it cannot be exploited to overcome disagreement, since the latter is radical, permitting no compromise. What must be exploited is just the desire of each participant to reach his own conclusions. A conclusion has no philosophical use if it is not reached freely. To be philosophically useful, it must represent the unconstrained attempt on the part of its advocate to fulfill his obligation to defend and clarify his position. Thus philosophical discussion is, in effect, a collaborative effort to maintain the conditions under which disagreement is possible. If it has arisen from an initial disagreement engendered by valid arguments to incompatible conclusions, it can proceed only by inviting further valid arguments from its

participants, because it is precisely by employing valid arguments
that each participant achieves the perfect exercise of his right to
reach his own conclusions. This account may suggest a kind of
monadism of philosophical positions — a plurality of positions,
each obeying its own inner law of development but wholly incapable of interacting with the others. In fact, however, it contains the germ of what I want to say about the ways in which
philosophical positions do interact. Interaction of this type, which
I have already referred to as "philosophical controversy," is possible only because philosophical discussion, in order to maintain
itself, must *exploit* the desire of each participant to reach his own
conclusions, and must *invite* him to argue validly. When the
motive to maintain the discussion is lacking, philosophical positions do, in fact, tend to become monadistically isolated from
each other; and this isolation owes itself to the radical nature of
their disagreements with each other. When it is present, on the
other hand, the disagreements are no less radical, but it is possible for the partisan of one position to invite a partisan of another to develop through unconstrained argument the consequences of a statement the latter has made. Since such consequences may prove to be an unexpected source of embarrass-
ment to the individual who develops them, it is an effective technique of philosophical controversy to invite one's opponent to
come to his own conclusions. Indeed, in the absence of the possibility of compromise, it is the only effective technique.

The success of the rhetorical speaker will depend upon the
extent to which there are beliefs, attitudes, prejudices, or premises
constituting an initial area of agreement on the part of his audience. Thus the speaker whose audience is most uniform in membership is likely to have the greatest chance of success. The
audience of rhetoric is therefore essentially limited. It is unlikely
that there are any statements that mankind as a whole could be
persuaded to accept, because it is unlikely that there is any area
of agreement to which all men would subscribe. The view has
been taken, however, that there are arguments addressed to mankind as a whole; to wit, the ones employed by the philosopher.[3]

---

[3] See Perelman and Olbrechts-Tyteca, *Rhétorique et Philosophie* (Paris,
Presses Universitaires de France, 1952) and *Traité de l'Argumentation*
(*ibid.*, 1958)

Such a view has the same source as the view of philosophical argumentation that I have been taking in this chapter: both arise from the feeling that the arguments employed by the philosopher are somehow different from those the persuasive speaker employs. But here, I think, the similarity ends. There are, in my opinion, two basic difficulties with the view that philosophical arguments are addressed to mankind as a whole. First, it has not been made clear how mankind as a whole could constitute an audience or what the philosopher could be intending to accomplish by addressing such an audience. According to the authors who take the view in question, the audience that the philosopher addresses has, in the last analysis, only an ideal existence: "We invent a model of man — the incarnation of reason . . . which we seek to convince, and which varies with our knowledge of other men, or other civilizations, or other systems of thought, with what we take to be incontrovertible facts or objective truths."[4] If certain individuals remain unmoved by his solicitations, the philosopher's only recourse is to regard them as irrational and thus as excluded from the ideal audience that he supposes himself to be addressing. In so doing, he substitutes the idea of an elite audience for that of a universal one. We seem to be left with the tautology that the philosopher addresses the audience that he addresses. But this has no tendency to show that the audience that the philosopher does address is mankind as a whole. Nor does it clearly indicate what transaction the philosopher is undertaking with his audience. What does it mean to "convince" a model that one has invented?

The second difficulty is that the radical nature of philosophical disagreement seems to diminish the force of the contention that the arguments of philosophers are addressed to a universal audience. If disagreement plays the fundamental role in philosophical argument that I have ascribed to it, then the audience of such argument, like the audience of rhetorical argument, must be limited. What distinguishes one limited audience of philosophical argumentation from another is the impossibility of resolving the issues between the two audiences by compromise. In this situation, the arguments effective against one audience would seem pointless to the other. It would appear that no philosophi-

---

[4] *Rhétorique et Philosophie,* p. 22

cal arguments addressed to mankind as a whole could be effective. This again raises a question about the point of saying that they are so addressed.

It has been objected that my characterization of philosophical argumentation emphasizes criticism or polemic, and that if I had paid proper attention to arguments of a constructive type, my results would have been compatible with the contention that the latter are addressed to a universal audience.[5] Now I admit the importance of the distinction between critical and constructive philosophical argumentation. I shall try to show later what role this distinction plays in my own analysis of philosophical argumentation. But for the moment, it has no role. Throughout this chapter what I have been attempting to characterize is philosophical discussion in general, whether critical or constructive in intent. I have tried to exhibit such discussion as the response to an obligation to amplify and defend. I see no reason why such a response would necessarily be confined either to criticism or to constructive elaboration. Both activities are appropriate to an obligation of the sort that I have in mind. Nor is there any reason why constructive arguments should, any less than critical arguments, constitute an effort to maintain the conditions of disagreement — an effort, that is, to invite the audience to reach its own conclusions. A constructive conclusion to which an audience acquiesces merely because it has been persuaded to do so is as philosophically useless as a critical conclusion reached under the same circumstances.

There is, nonetheless, an appealing quality in the idea that philosophical arguments are addressed to a universal audience. For this is a way of recapitulating the agelong theme that philosophy is fundamentally an exercise of reason. I do not take exception to this theme. I want only to raise the question whether reason must involve universality in the way it has usually been supposed to. There may be truths reached by reasoning that are equally acceptable to all rational beings. But if such truths exist, they are entirely without content. My view, however, is that the results of philosophical reasoning have content. Hence reason in its philosophical use cannot be universal.

---

[5] See Perelman, "Reply to Henry W. Johnstone, Jr.," *Philosophy and Phenomenological Research*, Vol. XVI, 1955, p. 246

V

The Validity of Philosophical Arguments — I

Much of what I have written so far would be pointless if the notion of a valid philosophical argument did not make sense, or if it were impossible for any philosophical argument to be valid. It would be pointless, for example, to discuss the relativity of truth to argument in philosophy if all the arguments for or against a given philosophical statement could be dismissed as invalid and thus as insufficient to establish the truth or falsity of the statement. It would be equally pointless to speak of an obligation to argue validly, rather than merely persuasively, if the obligation could never be met. Accordingly, I shall turn directly to the question whether valid philosophical arguments are possible.

It is well to begin by considering the standard method of dealing with this question. This method rests upon the assumption that the validity of any argument depends only upon its form. Once the form of an argument has been laid out, its validity can be determined by inspection or calculation or at least by some effective method. Thus if any philosophical arguments are of the requisite form, these, and these alone, will be valid philosophical arguments.

Valid arguments may, of course, assume any of a number of different forms. Contemporary logic, in fact, makes it clear that this number is indefinitely large. Perhaps the only feature common to all the forms that a valid argument may assume is also

common to most invalid arguments. This is the possibility of
making a sharp distinction between the premise or premises of
the argument and its conclusion. For the standard distinction between valid and invalid arguments seems to presuppose the common possibility of setting the premises of any argument on one
side and its conclusion on the other.

The question arises whether it is possible to lay out a philosophical argument with the premises on one side and the conclusion on the other without doing an injustice to the argument.
One reason for thinking that this is not possible is a phenomenon
to which Gilbert Ryle has called attention. When a philosopher
attempts to argue from explicit premises, "the debate instantly
moves back a step. The philosophical point at issue is seen to
be lodged . . . in those pretended premises themselves."[1] An example of what Ryle has in mind here is provided by one of Plato's
arguments for the immortality of the soul. I shall suggest which
argument I mean by misrepresenting it in the following way:

> The soul is simple.
> Whatever is simple cannot dissolve.
> Therefore, the soul cannot dissolve.

This syllogism is a misrepresentation because it immediately
raises a question that the argument actually used by Plato does
not raise immediately, if at all: to wit, "What possible reason is
there for supposing that the soul is, in fact, simple?" The syllo-
gistic formulation I have given evokes this question so promptly
and irrepressibly that it altogether lacks the force of the original
argument that it misrepresents. Only a complete and critical
reading of this original[2] could show what force it does have. But
it is clear that one of the reasons why Plato's argument is more
forceful than my syllogism is that the statement "The soul is
simple" does not function as an explicit premise capable of being
asserted independently of all other considerations. It is instead
inextricably interwoven with a large number of assumptions and
statements which together constitute an important part of Plato's
systematic doctrine. So if I have misrepresented Plato's argu-

---

[1] "Proofs in Philosophy," *Revue Internationale de Philosophie*, 1954,
p. 152

[2] *Phaedo*, 78b-84b

ment, I have not done so in a way that is readily corrigible. Indeed, if one were to set out to formulate the argument in such a way that the standard method could be used to determine its validity, it is difficult to see how one could, in principle, do a better job than the one I have done. More ultimate premises allegedly justifying "The soul is simple" could no doubt be introduced; but these would just raise further debilitating questions, so that to introduce such premises could not, in principle, overcome the defects of my formulation. In any event, syllogisms very much like mine are often used in commentaries on Plato and other philosophers.[3]

One point that should not be allowed to escape notice is that the syllogism through which I managed to misrepresent Plato's argument is valid from the point of view of the standard approach to validity. (To avoid such circumlocutions from now on, I shall simply say that an argument valid from this point of view is *formally* valid.) Yet it is without force. I juxtapose these two observations because there is something anomalous in the notion of an argument of which both observations could at the same time be true. In the case of most formally valid arguments either the question of force does not arise at all, or else the arguments are forceful. When a formally valid argument is presented as a schema, making it clear that the truth or falsity of premises or conclusion is irrelevant to the evaluation of the argument, the question of force does not arise. It makes no sense, for example, to ask whether "All M is P and all S is M, so all S is P" is a forceful argument or not. On the other hand, when any weight is attached to the claim that the premises of a formally valid argument are true, the force of the argument will depend upon to what extent the audience to which the argument is addressed is willing to "go along with" this claim. Thus "All men are mortal and Socrates is a man, so Socrates is mortal" has a force that it would lack if there were any doubt about the truth of its premises. It is well to distinguish the situation in which the truth of a premise is open to doubt from that in which the premise is assumed tentatively. A rigorous proof is a formally valid argument whose premises are postulates or are derived from postu-

---

[3] See, for example, Grube, *Plato's Thought* (Boston, Beacon Press, 1958) pp. 126-7

lates. Postulates are assumed tentatively rather than asserted
with finality, but to say this is not to say that they are subject
to doubt. To doubt a postulate would be no longer to treat it
as a postulate, because the doubt would presuppose a set of assumptions displacing it from its role as a postulate. A rigorous
proof, however, can have force; indeed, this is part of the meaning of saying that it is rigorous. Among formally valid arguments
with respect to which the question of force arises at all, only those
lack force whose premises, while claimed to be true, are in fact
open to doubt. But since the truth of a philosophical premise can
always be doubted, all formally valid philosophical arguments
will lack force. So the notion of formal validity does not seem
to be of much use in answering the question whether valid philosophical arguments are possible. The very attempt to set up a
philosophical argument in such a way as to make it possible to
ascertain whether it is formally valid or not seems inevitably to
result in a misrepresentation of the argument.

No further progress can be made until it has been decided
whether validity must necessarily be construed as formal validity.
There are several reasons for thinking that it need not be so construed. One reason is that it would be difficult, to say the least,
to give an unexceptionable account of what is meant by "formal
validity." The forms that arguments must possess in order to be
formally valid vary widely from one formal system to another,
as well as from one philosophy of logic (intuitionism, formalism,
etc.) to another, and whether a nontrivial statement of what is
common to all these forms could be given is doubtful. If we were
to insist that all valid arguments be formally valid, we would not
really know what we were insisting upon besides the distinguish-
ability of the premises from the conclusion. This feature in itself,
however, would not help us to separate valid from invalid arguments.

A perhaps stronger reason is the following: Let $F_i(S_j)$ be
the ith form (argument-schema) within formal system or philosophy of logic S_j such that any argument possessing this form is
valid. Then we can enumerate all possible forms of valid arguments as

$$F_1(S_1), F_2(S_1), \ldots F_1(S_2), F_2(S_2), \ldots F_m(S_n).$$

Now concerning any member $F_i(S_j)$ of this series we can always ask with perfect propriety, "Is an argument of form F_1 (S_j) valid?" It makes sense, for example, to ask whether a syllogism of the form AAA in the First Figure is valid. This shows that "valid" cannot *mean* "having form F_1 (S_j)." If it did, our question would sound like the question "Are all squares rectangles?" which can be answered simply by inspecting the meanings of the terms and which thus does not arise for a person already acquainted with these meanings. But the question "Is an argument of the form F_1 (S_j) valid?" does constantly arise for people engaged in formal logic. So while some arguments may be valid by virtue of the form they possess, their validity cannot reduce simply to their possession of this form.

A third reason for refusing to identify validity with formal validity is that there are many people unacquainted with the notion of formal validity who are perfectly able to recognize arguments as valid or invalid. One does not have to take a course in formal logic in order to learn how to reason. The distinction between valid and invalid arguments was known long before the area of formal validity was explored. It is almost a platitude, for example, that the argument "Horses are animals, so the heads of horses are the heads of animals" was known to be valid long before any means was discovered of exhibiting the form this argument possesses by virtue of which it is valid. It has recently been claimed[4] that logical-sounding arguments in ordinary discourse borrow their prestige from formal logic. But this seems to put the matter the wrong way around. Formal logic arose at least partly as the critique of logical-sounding arguments in ordinary discourse; for example, of those used by the Sophists.

The fact that validity antedates formal validity suggests that if we wish to give an adequate account of validity, we must return to its pre-formal version. Such a return will be made easier if we remind ourselves that the adjective "valid" as it is ordinarily used can modify nouns other than "argument." It is perfectly proper to speak of a valid criticism, a valid objection, or a valid judgment. For that matter, we can speak of a valid passport or a valid contract, for even these expressions belong to the same family. Both a valid criticism and a valid passport are somehow

---

[4] By Perelman and Olbrechts-Tyteca in *Traité de l'Argumentation* (Paris, 1958) pp. 259-260

relevant: the passport to the travel plans of its holder, and the criticism to the thing or person criticized. A valid criticism *has* force and a valid passport is *in* force; this may be a pun, but I am not sure that it is, because there is something in common between these two uses of the word "force," neither of which has anything to do with the product of mass and acceleration. Conversely, an invalid passport — one that has expired, for example — is no longer relevant or in force, and an invalid criticism may be irrelevant in the sense of missing the point; in any event, we say that it "lacks force." These two notions of relevance and force are, I shall maintain, the root ideas common at least to valid arguments, criticisms, objections, and judgments, even if not to valid passports or contracts.

I am not sure that the notions of relevance and force are altogether separable. An at least partial separation can be accomplished, however, by comparing a defect of relevance with a defect of force. Suppose I wish to attack a proposal to levy a sales tax in my state. I may criticize the proposal on the grounds that a hardship will be imposed on many people who cannot afford to pay more for food than they are now paying. But if it is not in fact intended that the proposed tax should apply to purchases of food, my criticism is clearly irrelevant and so invalid. I may, on the other hand, condemn the proposal by simply pointing out that rich and poor will be taxed alike. Assume that this criticism is relevant; that is, that the proponents of the tax do envisage that the same taxes will apply to rich and poor alike. In this case, my criticism merely reports one of the admitted features of the thing I am trying to criticize. Unless I also show why I think it wrong that rich and poor should be taxed alike, the criticism altogether lacks force. Of course, one can forcefully criticize a personage, institution, or proposal by making what appears to be no more than an accurate report upon it, provided that one uses irony or innuendo with sufficient skill. I am thinking now, however, of a genuine report that simply repeats what is admitted to be the case. Neither a criticism consisting simply in such a report nor a criticism based upon an inaccurate report could be valid.

It seems clear that no argument lacking relevance can have force. On the other hand, an argument could have relevance without having force. These two statements summarize all that I have discovered about the relationship between relevance and force.

Traditional logic has taken cognizance of the two modes of invalidity in question by dismissing some arguments as formally invalid and others as question-begging. The project of exhibiting the forms of valid arguments is, in effect, an attempt to state a sufficient condition for the relevance of the premises of an argument to its conclusion. If, for example, an argument is of the form "All M is P and all S is M, so all S is P," then, however the premises and conclusion are instantiated (barring equivocations), the former are guaranteed to be relevant to the latter. There is nothing to suggest, however, that any *necessary* conditions for relevance could result from the accomplishment of this project. It is well known that even when an inductive argument is formally invalid, its premises can be relevant to its conclusion.

The notion of a question-begging argument has not been studied by contemporary logicians as extensively as it ought to be, but it is clear how this notion is treated in traditional logic. From this point of view, a *petitio principii* is to be rejected, not because the premises are irrelevant to the conclusion, but because they are relevant to the point of identity. When one of the premises is simply the conclusion itself in a disguised form, the argument lacks force. Yet any such argument would, of course, be formally valid, for the simple reason that "*p*, therefore *p*" is a tautology.

There is a certain anomaly, however, in having to say that a question-begging argument is valid. We would not normally say that a question-begging criticism was a valid criticism. This anomaly seems to result from the tendency in formal logic to identify validity with relevance, and to neglect the notion of force. The force of an argument has been treated as simply a matter of the truth of its premises, and the question of whether the premises of an argument are true has been altogether dissociated from the question of whether the argument is valid. As I have already indicated, I see no objection to treating the force of an argument as a function of the truth of its premises where the validity of the argument does in fact rest upon formal considerations alone, as in the case of a rigorous proof. But there are other cases in which the force of an argument is not a function of the truth of its premises. Here validity itself is a function of force as well as of relevance. The *petitio* is an example, because even when its conclusion-anticipating premise happens to be true, the argument gains no force from that circumstance.

If validity is not to be equated with formal validity, this seems to open the door to the possibility of valid philosophical arguments. I should like now to give some examples of philosophical arguments that I regard as valid. In each case I shall indicate why I think the argument is valid, and why I feel that its validity cannot be analyzed as a case of formal validity.

One of the arguments used by Eudoxus in the attempt to show that pleasure is the chief good was that "any good thing — e.g., just or temperate conduct — is made more desirable by the addition of pleasure."[5] But Aristotle called attention to the fact that an argument of exactly the same type can be constructed to show that the chief good is *not* pleasure. For, as Plato had already argued, "the pleasant life is more desirable with wisdom than without,"[6] so that wisdom would seem to be the chief good. Of course, this argument is not really isomorphic with that of Eudoxus unless Aristotle intends to suggest, with Plato's authority or without it, that if wisdom be added to *any* good thing — not just to the pleasant life — the result is more desirable. Plato's authority is, in any event, readily forthcoming. Let us assume that this is what Aristotle did mean to suggest.

On this assumption, Aristotle's criticism is devastating. If Eudoxus did actually use the argument ascribed to him by Aristotle, it is difficult to see how he could conscionably continue to use it in the face of this criticism. There does not even seem to be any way in which he could *revise* it to meet the criticism. Any appropriate revision would require some proviso to the effect that pleasure is not really rendered more desirable by the addition of any other good (for example, wisdom), even though it might appear to be. But the inclusion of such a proviso would destroy the peculiar argumentative force of Eudoxus' argument, for the proviso itself would be tantamount to the simple state-

---

[5] Aristotle, *Nicomachean Ethics*, 1172[b] 24-26. Translated by Philip Wheelwright in *Aristotle* (New York, Odyssey Press, 1951) p. 254
[6] *Ibid.*, 29-30

ment that pleasure *is* the chief good, and the argument as a whole could then be impugned as question-begging. In view of Aristotle's attack, then, Eudoxus ought to have withdrawn his argument.

There can be no question that Aristotle's criticism of Eudoxus' argument is relevant to what it attacks. It would be extravagant to hold that Aristotle in any way misses the point of Eudoxus' argument. Indeed, the very force of Aristotle's criticism is just the result of the way in which that criticism makes use of the point of Eudoxus' argument. No criticism can be maximally forceful unless it is exactly relevant. Of course, a question-begging criticism would be exactly relevant but of minimum force. But Aristotle's criticism, far from begging the question, has maximum force. The origin of this force is the seriousness of Eudoxus' commitment to the principle of reasoning that he has used in trying to prove that pleasure is the chief good. If he is serious, then he must be willing to maintain this principle. But if he maintains it, then Aristotle can overthrow him by using exactly the same principle. So the force of Aristotle's criticism derives from the fact that Aristotle uses Eudoxus' seriousness to undercut the very thing about which he is serious — he shows that Eudoxus has defeated his *own* purpose.

Aristotle's criticism of Eudoxus' argument is itself, of course, an argument. It is, in fact, an *argumentum ad hominem,* since it attacks Eudoxus in terms of his own principles. Later I shall discuss the general properties of *argumenta ad hominem.* For the moment, I want only to make the point that it would not be rash to characterize Aristotle's argument, involving maximum force and exact relevance,[7] as valid; but it would be at least misleading to call it *formally* valid.

Let me try to amplify this point. When it is forceful, a formally valid argument establishes a conclusion. But Aristotle's argument does not establish any conclusion, or even *claim* to establish one. In particular, Aristotle does not here conclude, nor attempt to conclude, that pleasure is *not* the chief good. He

---

[7] I say that an argument itself, rather than just a set of premises, has relevance (to a conclusion) because I cannot sharply distinguish between premises and conclusion. This consideration also accounts for the expression ". . . obligated to accept the conclusion, in view of the argument" (not ". . . in view of the premises") that I used throughout Chapter IV.

merely says that we *could* use an argument similar to that of
Eudoxus to show that pleasure is not the chief good.[8] He does
not attack Eudoxus' conclusion; he attacks only his way of reaching a conclusion. This brings me to an alternative way in which
it might be thought possible to construe Aristotle's argument as
formally valid. The argument to the effect that someone else's
way of reaching a conclusion constitutes an invalid argument
might itself be a formally valid argument, of the form "All arguments of such-and-such a form are invalid; this argument is of
that form; therefore this argument is invalid." But Aristotle's
criticism of Eudoxus is far from being a case in point. For one
thing, Aristotle is not arguing *about* Eudoxus' argument; he is
arguing *in terms of* Eudoxus' argument. In any event, he does
not reject the latter as formally invalid. Such a rejection could
be justified only after the logical relations among the terms of the
argument had been specified and the suppressed premises, if any,
explicitly stated. Aristotle provides us with no such exegesis. He
is not interested in seeing whether the argument is, in fact, valid,
formally or otherwise. His concern is hypothetical only: "*If*
Eudoxus' argument is valid," he is saying, "*then* so is Plato's."
Perhaps, then, Aristotle is trying to prove the invalidity of Eudoxus' argument by means of a *modus tollens*. But the fact is that
he never even stops to consider whether Plato's argument is valid
or not. So perhaps he is trying to prove the invalidity of the form
common to Plato's and Eudoxus' arguments by showing that
arguments having this form in common can have mutually inconsistent conclusions. This hypothesis comes the closest of any that
I have so far considered to fitting all the facts. But there is one
fact that it still does not fit. If Aristotle's argument were intended
as a *reductio* of the kind I have suggested, it would be an attack
upon the validity of Plato's argument as well as upon that of
Eudoxus. It is clear, however, that it is Eudoxus whom Aristotle
is attacking, not Plato. In this particular passage, Aristotle regards Plato as an ally. He uses Plato's argument as a means of
exerting pressure against Eudoxus. But he certainly could not

---

8 Perhaps scholars will dispute this point. But Aristotle did not, at any
rate, *have* to conclude at this point that pleasure is not the chief good.
Whether he actually concluded it or not has no effect upon the force of
his argument.

do this if he were at the same time raising a question about the validity of Plato's argument. One cannot use pressure if at the same time one causes the pressure to collapse.

I do not wish to deny the possibility of attacking the form common to Plato's argument and that of Eudoxus by setting up the *reductio* I have considered. All that I am denying is the propriety of analyzing in this way the argument used by Aristotle to attack Eudoxus. I hope that my comments have lent some plausibility to the contention that Aristotle's argument is not *about* Eudoxus' argument, but is rather *in terms of* it. One talks *about* arguments in treatises on logic or rhetoric. The very fact that this is a treatise on ethics, not logic or rhetoric, creates a certain presumption. Of course, even in a treatise on ethics one can point out that a certain ethical argument is invalid. But as I have already tried to show, Aristotle does not seem interested in the validity of Eudoxus' argument. Instead of *attacking* Eudoxus' argument at all, he *uses* Eudoxus' argument to attack Eudoxus.

The next example that I want to consider is Berkeley's argument to the effect that it is hopeless to appeal to external bodies in the attempt to explain the causes of our ideas: "For, though we give the materialists their external bodies, they by their own confession are never the nearer to knowing how our ideas are produced; since they own themselves unable to comprehend in what manner body can act upon spirit."[9] I shall maintain that this is a valid argument. It is directly relevant to the position it attacks. Because it is relevant, it can use the very energy with which the materialists have defended their thesis to overthrow that thesis. There is no doubt that it does overthrow it. In view of Berkeley's argument, it is clear that his opponents ought either to reverse their stand regarding the incomprehensibility of how body acts upon spirit, or else give up appealing to external bodies in the attempt to explain how our ideas are produced. Thus Berkeley's argument has maximal force. When an argument combines exact relevance with maximal force, I do not see how one can avoid supposing it to be valid.

If this valid argument were formally valid, it would require at least one clearly discernible premise. Perhaps the premise on

---

[9] *Principles,* Sec. 19

which Berkeley's conclusion is based is something like "It is incomprehensible how body acts upon spirit." But anyone who attempts to *prove* Berkeley's conclusion on the basis of this premise (and perhaps some others) is almost certain to fail. For there are sure to be many people to whom the premise is unacceptable. It is difficult to show that there is absolutely no way to comprehend a situation; perhaps the way to comprehend it is just elusive. Thus it may be tempting to reply to the alleged premise by *explaining* how body acts upon spirit. I say this as a reminder of the phenomenon noted by Ryle: Whenever philosophers argue from explicit premises, "the debate instantly moves back a step. The philosophical point at issue is seen to be lodged . . . in those pretended premises themselves." Philosophical premises can always be regarded with suspicion, and a justification for the suspicion can always be found when necessary. But if we review the argument actually used by Berkeley, we shall find that this suspicion-engendered backward step from conclusion to premises does not, in fact, occur. For it is Berkeley's antagonists themselves — the "materialists" — who have supplied the premise. They have themselves pronounced it incomprehensible how body acts upon spirit. Berkeley's argument does nothing more than exhibit a consequence of this pronouncement.

While Berkeley's argument against the "materialists" and Aristotle's argument against Eudoxus are at least generically similar, in the sense that both are valid philosophical arguments and neither is formally valid, there may seem to be important differences between them. For one thing, it would be pointless to discuss the Ryle phenomenon in connection with Aristotle's argument. Not only does Aristotle not argue from explicit premises, but also it is implausible to hypothesize any explicit premises from which he *might* be arguing. (We did hypothesize the premise "Eudoxus' argument is of such-and-such a form [and so is invalid]"; but this turned out to be implausible at first blush.) The reason for this situation is that Aristotle is primarily concerned with an argument rather than with a statement. Berkeley, on the other hand, is primarily occupied in attacking a statement; to wit, the statement that we can explain the causes of our ideas in terms of external bodies. It is usually more natural to attribute responsibility for a particular statement to a particular thinker than it is to attribute responsibility for a particular argument to a particular thinker. A thinker *makes* a statement, but *uses* an argument. Thus it is more natural to suppose that an argument is *ad hominem* when it concerns a statement that a thinker has made than when it concerns an argument that he has used. For this reason, the *ad hominem* force of Berkeley's argument may be more obvious than that of Aristotle's argument. But the difference is, in fact, superficial. Aristotle's argument attacks Eudoxus' argument not just as an argument of a common and interesting type, but as the specific instrument of a specific point of view. Aristotle's polemic would have been pointless if Eudoxus (or someone else) had not actually argued in this way, for it would then have constituted an attack on a straw man. But attacks on straw men are deplored only when attacks on flesh-and-blood men are accepted. This is one way of expressing the reason Aristotle's argument is *ad hominem*. It is not any less *ad hominem* than is Berkeley's argument. Berkeley is attacking the propounders of a statement not as persons but as promulgators of a point of view with which the statement is incompatible. Berkeley does not here even name any "materialists," although Aristotle does name Eudoxus. Neither argument achieves its force as a result either of discussing personalities or of appealing to an objective state of affairs, like the fact that such-and-such an argument is formally invalid. Both are equally *ad hominem*.

One way of describing the force of Aristotle's argument against Eudoxus is to say that it shows that Eudoxus' own argument is self-defeating. Analogously, Berkeley's argument shows that the position of the "materialists" is self-defeating. Both arguments make the point that what is under attack has undercut itself. Thus both refer something to itself with damaging effect. Yet the self-referential aspect of each of these two arguments is probably not so obvious as it is in the case of certain other valid philosophical arguments. In order to highlight this aspect, I turn to a third argument. This one, unlike the previous two, cannot be assigned any definite authorship. It has been used by a number of authors, and the question of historical priority does not seem to me to be of much interest. The argument is an attempt to show that the naturalistic view of knowledge renders itself untenable. For, as a recent version of this argument points out,

"In . . . deriving mind and knowledge from nature, as science conceives it," the naturalist

> . . . must assume that his own account of nature is true. But on his premises, the truth of this account, like that of any other bit of knowledge, is merely the function of the adjustment of the organism to its environment, and thus has no more significance than any other adjustment. Its sole value is its survival value. This entire conception of knowledge refutes itself.[10]

This argument seems to me to exemplify *par excellence* the convergence of relevance and force to be found in valid philosophical arguments. But I shall postpone any elaboration of this point until somewhat later, and proceed directly to the question of whether, if valid, the argument can be formally valid. This question can be answered very simply. Whenever the argument under discussion has been judged according to formal criteria of validity, it has been rejected as formally invalid.[11] The basis of this rejection has been one version or another of the doctrine of the stratification of types, or of the doctrine according to which there exists a hierarchy of languages. Thus it is maintained that the apparently paradoxical or self-refuting character of the naturalistic view of knowledge is an illusion that results from inattention to the requirements of stratification. If the statement, "All knowledge, including this, is merely the function of the adjustment of the organism to its environment," appears paradoxical, this is only because one has failed to see that "this knowledge" belongs to a higher type than "all knowledge." But once the type levels are properly distinguished, the argument against the naturalistic view of knowledge loses all its force. Since the argument commits an equivocation, it is formally invalid.

But this indictment of the argument against naturalism seems itself the result of inattentiveness. What needs to be attended to more closely is the fact that there are only two reasons for distinguishing among types. One is to avoid logical contradictions, and the other is to represent real differences in scope or abstract-

---

10 Wilbur Marshall Urban, *Beyond Realism and Idealism* (London, Allen and Unwin, 1949; and New York, Macmillan) p. 236

11 Perhaps Fitch would not reject this argument as formally invalid. But the fact that it is closely similar to arguments that he considers to be *argumenta ad hominem* suggests that he would not consider it formally valid, either. See "Self-Reference in Philosophy," *Mind,* Vol. 55, 1946, pp. 64-73

ness among propositions. I shall try to show that neither of these reasons can possibly be relevant to the situation I am now discussing.

First, the paradox of the naturalist who asserts that all knowledge is the function of the adjustment of the organism to its environment is not a logical paradox. The statement that knowledge of the truth of naturalism has a naturalistic explanation is not formally inconsistent. Indeed, there are occasions when it serves a useful purpose to make such a statement. To the biographer, for example, it may be of importance to show that a certain naturalistic philosopher adopted his views as a mode of adjustment to his environment. The paradox arises only from the fact that it is the naturalist himself who makes the statement. For in so doing, he confesses that he made the statement only because he had to — in order to adjust to his own environment. Thus the question of the truth or falsity of the statement cannot really arise. Yet the naturalist is surely claiming that his statement is true. He is in the predicament of a man who claims that he is responsible for his own statement that he is not responsible for his own statements.

It is indeed a paradox to say, "I am not responsible for my own statements." But this paradox differs only by a personal pronoun from the nonparadoxical statement, "You are not responsible for your own statements," which has obvious uses. This possibility of constructing a nonparadoxical statement out of a paradoxical one by replacing pronouns is associated with what are called "pragmatic paradoxes." In general, a pragmatic paradox is a statement whose credibility is undercut by the act of uttering it; for the utterance has implications that the statement itself does not have. To utter, "I never use correct English," I must use correct English. But the fact that I must is not implied by the statement itself. Similarly, the statement that I am not responsible for my own statements does not in itself imply that I am; only its utterance does. This feature of pragmatic paradoxes is sufficient to distinguish them altogether from the logical paradoxes engendered by the confusion of types; for the statement, "The class of all classes that are not members of themselves is not a member of itself," does imply its own contradictory, whether it is uttered or not.

The argument against the naturalistic view of knowledge, then, does not ignore any distinction of types that must be made in order to overcome a logical contradiction; for there is no logical contradiction to be overcome. But perhaps the argument will still be impugned for overlooking a real distinction, contradiction or no. It may be said that the knowledge that all knowledge is the function of the adjustment of the organism to its environment is not itself such a function, but belongs to a higher and substantially different type. This distinction can be indicated by subscripts: I have knowledge$_2$ that all knowledge$_1$ is a function of adjustment. Put this way, the paradox seems to disappear; for I need only assert that I am responsible$_2$ for the statement that I am not responsible$_1$ for my own statements.

But can the distinction between knowledge$_1$ and knowledge$_2$ ultimately be maintained? In most cases, it obviously can. I know$_2$ that my knowledge$_1$ of the land areas of the continents arises from the latest almanac. In such a case, my knowledge$_2$ is the theory or explanation of my knowledge$_1$, and is distinguishable from it in answering to a different procedure of verification. There is, in other words, an objective way of distinguishing knowledge$_1$ from knowledge$_2$. Certainly, neither is a special case of the other.

By what mark, however, can the naturalist distinguish his knowledge$_1$ from his knowledge$_2$, other than by his mere wish to withhold from knowledge$_2$ the criticism that he applies to knowledge$_1$? What is there to prevent us from treating the former (i.e., the naturalist's knowledge that his knowledge$_1$ is a function of his own adjustment to his environment) as simply a special case of the latter (i.e., the knowledge that he claims is a function of his environment)? We have only the naturalist's word for it that this cannot be done. And we know that he is far from being a disinterested witness.

There is, then, no genuine distinction between the scope or abstractness of the naturalist's knowledge$_1$ and that of his knowledge$_2$ to justify the appeal to a stratification of types. It follows that there is no justification for invoking types at all in connection with the attempt to discredit the argument against the naturalistic view of knowledge. Yet both this argument and many similar ones are likely to inspire particularly stubborn resistance.

Even those who are willing to admit that the argument in question violates no canon of type-theory are likely to condemn it as invalid. They may well express their condemnation by using pejoratively a phrase that I have tended to use honorifically; namely, "*argumentum ad hominem*." For it is tempting to object that the argument proves nothing about the naturalistic view of knowledge; it is merely an attempt to discredit the testimony of anyone who testifies on behalf of this view.

The only hope of meeting this objection is to show not only that valid *argumenta ad hominem* are possible as well as invalid ones, but also that a valid *argumentum ad hominem* can properly be used to attack a philosophical view as well as to discredit the testimony of those who advocate the view. It is best to begin with a definition of "*argumentum ad hominem*" on which both sides can agree. In all likelihood, Whately's definition meets this requirement. "In the '*argumentum ad hominem*,'" he states, "the conclusion which actually is established, is not the absolute and general one in question, but relative and particular; viz., not that 'such and such is the fact,' but that '*this* man is bound to admit it, in conformity to his principles of reasoning, or consistency with his own conduct, situation,' &c."[12] Thus there is no difficulty in supposing that an *argumentum ad hominem* actually establishes a conclusion, although there may be some difficulty in being sure what conclusion it actually establishes. But an argument that actually establishes the conclusion that it claims to establish is clearly a valid argument, while an argument that claims to establish a conclusion that is, in fact, independent of the conclusion that it actually establishes is invalid. Accordingly, an *argumentum ad hominem*, like any other argument, will be valid when it establishes the conclusion it claims to establish, and invalid when it establishes a conclusion independent of this.

---

[12] Richard Whately, *Elements of Logic* (New York, William Jackson, 1838), p. 196. It should be recognized that Whately's definition has no relevance to the contemporary usage of "*argumentum ad hominem*" to denote mudslinging. But this usage is not at issue in the present context, since no one accuses the critic of the naturalistic view of knowledge of engaging in a mudslinging attack on the naturalist.

The phrase "*argumentum ad hominem*," as it was used at least prior to Whately's time, did not refer to a generally invalid type of argument. The use of it that I intend will be found, for instance, in Thomas Reid, *Essays on the Intellectual Powers of Man* (Edinburgh, 1785), Essay VI, Ch. IV.

There is no reason under the sun to suppose that an *argumentum ad hominem* must necessarily be invalid.

In order to bring out more clearly the conditions that must be met by a valid *argumentum ad hominem*, I want to consider some obviously invalid uses of arguments of this type. To an opponent who defends suicide, Schopenhauer says in *The Art of Controversy*,[13] "you may at once exclaim, 'Why don't you hang yourself?' Should he maintain that Berlin is an unpleasant place to live, you may say, 'Why don't you leave by the first train?' Some such claptrap is always possible."

Why is this "claptrap"? Only because the principle of reasoning or situation to which the would-be refuter calls attention is one in which his opponent has no essential stake. The distaste for Berlin may be only an idiosyncrasy. Or if it is a consistent motive, it may not be an ultimate one. Most men have purposes that take precedence over geographical considerations; perhaps such a purpose irresistibly detains this man in a Berlin that he nevertheless finds unpleasant. Similarly, he who argues for suicide is not likely to feel an irresistible urge for self-destruction; he may regard the need for suicide as contingent upon conditions, such as sacrifice or *Weltschmerz*, that he does not think of as being at all relevant to himself.

Suppose, however, that one's interlocutor does in fact feel an unconditional obligation to leave Berlin or to do away with himself. The argumentation ironically suggested by Schopenhauer would then be exactly relevant to the interlocutor's situation, and would have just the force of the obligation that he himself felt. The man who asserts that he is essentially bound to leave Berlin, and yet fails to leave it, is in a position of fundamental confusion. No logical canon is violated by a critic insofar as he merely points out this confusion.

Whether the argument against the naturalistic view of knowledge is a valid *argumentum ad hominem* or not depends upon whether the naturalist must be supposed to have an essential stake in the situation or principle of reasoning to which the argument calls attention or whether, on the contrary, this situation or principle is one to which he need not be committed, at least in

---

[13] Tr. by Bailey Saunders (London, Swan Somenschein & Co., 1896) p. 28

his role as a naturalist. In fact, he does have an essential stake. If he holds that *all* knowledge is a function of the adjustment of the organism to its environment and at the same time pleads that his own knowledge is an exception to this generalization, he cannot hope to be taken seriously. If he tries to extricate himself from this predicament by declaring that just *some* knowledge is a function of the adjustment of the organism to its environment, he is no longer advocating naturalism, but is only making a quite unexceptionable empirical statement. Thus the stake of the naturalist in his own situation is measured by his desire to be taken seriously and at the same time to be a naturalist.

The validity of the argument against the naturalist, like that of the argument against the man who does feel unconditionally bound to leave Berlin — and indeed like that of all the valid philosophical arguments I have so far considered — may be thought of as arising from a convergence of relevance and force. The relevance of the critic's assertion about the naturalist's knowledge to what the naturalist has himself asserted about knowledge in general seems unquestionable. The force of the argument is just the force of the obligation that the naturalist feels to make the assertion he does about knowledge in general.

I should like now to ask to what extent, if any, the argument I have been discussing is actually an attack on naturalism rather than merely an attack on the naturalist. The answer hinges on the intelligibility of the proposition that a philosophy might be true even though all of its proponents have been refuted. For if one proponent of the naturalistic view of knowledge can be refuted by *argumentum ad hominem,* all can. So the argument under discussion is a valid *argumentum ad hominem* not only when it is construed as a claim to discredit the testimony of particular naturalists, but also when it is regarded as a claim to refute naturalism itself.

This completes the remarks I had wanted to make about the present example of a philosophical argument. Like the others, it is valid but not formally valid. Like them, too, it is an *argumentum ad hominem.* Some of the aspects of valid philosophical arguments are more conspicuously present in this example than in the others — I refer especially to the self-referential aspect and to the suspicion that the argument may arouse once its *ad hominem* force becomes clear — but these aspects are also to some degree involved in the others. Indeed, I will go so far as to claim that all the aspects to which I have called attention are characteristics of all valid philosophical arguments. All that I can say in support of this claim is that it seems to me to be a direct consequence of a thesis that I defended in a previous chapter. If the truth or falsity of any philosophical statement is relative to the argument that establishes or disestablishes it, then, unlike the truth or falsity of a scientific statement, it is not relative to objective facts. Hence there is no *argumentum ad rem* to establish or disestablish any philosophical statement. This leaves open only the possibility of an *argumentum ad hominem*. But any valid *argumentum ad hominem* will be found to have the same characteristics as each of my examples has been found to have. It will exhibit the self-defeating nature of an argument or statement that it attacks. It will be directly relevant to this argument or statement. It will borrow its force from the energy with which what it attacks is asserted. And so on.

In this chapter, I have said a great deal about how philosophical arguments and statements can be disestablished, but so far almost nothing about how they can be established. What I have said on the latter point has been by indirection only. I pointed out that no philosophical conclusion can be established by arguing from explicit premises, for the premises of a philosophical argument cannot be altogether distinguished from the conclusion. It is time to amplify this point and to explain its bearing upon the properties of constructive philosophical arguments. To say that the premises cannot be distinguished from the conclusion is to say that the conclusion is the same as, or closely resembles, one or more of the premises. But an argument of which this is true is usually characterized as circular. It is my view that valid constructive arguments in philosophy must in fact be circular, for otherwise the Ryle phenomenon would be bound to occur, as it does not only in the case of my misrepresentation of Plato's argument, but also whenever the attempt has been made to "prove" philosophical conclusions by means of explicit postulates. Accordingly, I take the position that the argument of Plato's that I misrepresented was, as Plato actually expressed it, circular. In particular, I strongly suspect that in view of Plato's systematic doctrine "The soul is simple" means very much the same thing as "The soul cannot dissolve." I said previously that "The soul is simple" is inextricably interwoven with a large number of assumptions and statements, which together constitute an important part of Plato's systematic doctrine. Unless a person accepted at least that part of the doctrine, he could not accept the premise that the soul is simple. But the part of Plato's doctrine that one would have to accept in order to accept this premise would undoubtedly already include the thesis that the soul cannot dissolve.

Should Plato's argument, then, be dismissed as invalid? Shall we say that "circular" and "question-begging" mean the same, and that both circular and question-begging arguments ought to be dismissed on the grounds that, while they possess relevance, they lack force? It is clear that for an individual wholly unsympathetic to Plato's doctrine, Plato's argument for the immortality of the soul would have no force at all. Yet there are those for whom it might be forceful. A person vaguely and inarticulately committed to a generally platonistic point of view could very well be led, by means of Plato's argument, to see the bearing of his own commitment upon the question of the immortality of the soul. Such a person — not, after all, very much unlike the Simmias or the Cebes of the dialogue — would regard the argument as valid. Perhaps he would be right. In view of the developments in Chapter IV, there is nothing to prevent a philosophical argument from being valid for one person even though invalid for others. Any such argument will be valid insofar as it correctly develops consequences of the philosophical commitments of the individual or group to whom it is addressed. This is just as true of constructive arguments as it is of critical ones. There may be something strange in the claim that constructive arguments are addressed to individuals or particular groups. But in Chapter IV, I tried to show that no philosophical argument *could* be addressed to any audience whose membership is unlimited.

A somewhat more striking illustration of the position I am advocating with regard to constructive philosophical arguments is provided by Mill's "Proof of the Principle of Utility":

> The only proof capable of being given that an object is visible, is that people actually see it. The only proof that a sound is

audible, is that people hear it: and so of the other sources of our experience. In like manner, I apprehend, the sole evidence that it is possible to produce that anything is desirable, is that people do actually desire it. If the end which the utilitarian doctrine proposes to itself were not, in theory and in practice, acknowledged to be an end, nothing could ever convince any person that it was so. No reason can be given why the general happiness is desirable except that each person, so far as he believes it to be attainable, desires his own happiness.[14]

It is perhaps Mill's use of the word "proof," as much as any other factor, that has brought about the nearly universal rejection of this argument. As a proof, it suffers exactly the fate of all alleged proofs in philosophy. The premise that the desirable is what people actually desire has displaced the conclusion as the locus of the issue. This premise is impugned as equivocal. For "desirable" means not only "capable of being desired" (so the customary criticism runs) but also "worthy of being desired"; and it is only in this second sense of "desirable" that it is important for Mill to show that happiness is desirable. One does not prove that happiness is *worthy* of being desired merely by pointing to evidence that shows it *capable* of being desired.

Yet if Mill had not pretentiously labeled his argument a "proof," this criticism would miss the point. For a Utilitarian, there is clearly no sense of "desirable" over and above "capable of being desired." *Qua* Utilitarian, he cannot even conceive of a thing worthy of being desired but not capable of being desired. The words, to which he cannot attach any meaning, smack of Kantian a priorism, a position that Utilitarianism radically opposes. Thus Mill's argument is actually circular. The conclusion "Happiness is desirable" is very little different, if at all different, from the premise "Happiness is desired." At the same time, for a Utilitarian in the process of working out his position, as Mill was when he wrote this essay, the argument is not without force. The idea that "Happiness is desirable" means much the same as "Happiness is desired" might not have initially been clear to Mill. To use the argument would then be to explore a hitherto only partly articulated point of view. One result of using it would be to structure this point of view. All valid constructive philosophical arguments involve this element of feedback. They use the

---

[14] John Stuart Mill, *Utilitarianism,* Ch. IV

partial structure of a point of view to structure the point of view further. Feedback, of course, is a kind of circularity.[15]

A constructive philosophical argument, when valid, is very much like a valid *argumentum ad hominem*. The only important difference is that the philosopher using a constructive argument considers what he himself is bound to admit, in conformity to his own principles of reasoning or in consistency with his own conduct or situation, rather than considering what someone else is bound to admit. The constructive argument is thus essentially an *argumentum ad seipsum*.

From the point of view of analysis, constructive philosophical arguments seem to constitute a distinctive genus. That is, one can perfectly well analyze a given constructive philosophical argument without coming to the conclusion that the argument is not really constructive. Thus my analysis of Mill's argument took it for granted that Mill had something positive to say, and that his argument was part of the way in which he tried to say it. From a genetic point of view, however, Mill's exposition looks slightly different. It appears as just the articulation of a radical opposition to Kantian a priorism in ethics — an opposition that is more directly expressed in Mill's very able critique of Kant in the first chapter of his essay. This critique is a series of critical philosophical arguments. It is my view that every positive position in philosophy arises from a similar critique. It originates in a radical denial. Thus critical argumentation is genetically prior to constructive.

In addition to constructive and critical arguments — those that attempt to establish a conclusion, and those that attempt to disestablish one — there are defensive arguments, which are efforts to disarm criticism. The ideal defensive argument is the inverse of the ideal critical one: while the latter takes a defendant seriously in order to acquire its force and relevance from his own position, the former shows that a prosecutor has not taken the defendant seriously enough, so that his argument lacks either relevance or force or both. I shall try to explain and illustrate

---

[15] Further commentary on Mill's argument and the ways in which it has been criticized, along lines not unlike the one I have taken here, will be found in Norman Kretzmann's "Desire as a Proof of Desirability," *The Philosophical Quarterly*, 1958, pp. 246-258

this form of defensive argumentation in Chapter VII. No technical name has been given it, nor need any be; but in essence it consists of accusing one's critic of having begged the question. On the analogy of the statement that all valid philosophical arguments are *argumenta ad hominem*, it would be tidy if one could say that all invalid philosophical arguments are *petitiones principii*, but this cannot quite truly be said. For many irresponsibly invalid philosophical arguments are just amorphous cases of *non sequitur*. Perhaps it is true that all invalid philosophical arguments that are somehow still "responsible" or "respectable" are *petitiones principii*. But this raises the ugly question of the meaning of "respectability" in philosophy. In any event, the distinction I have in mind between a *petitio principii*, or question-begging argument, and a circular argument should now be clear. The *petitio* is a criticism that fails because it either appeals to what the defendant of the point of view being criticized has denied, or else it denies what he has appealed to. But the philosopher engaged in elaborating his own doctrine would simply not be in a position to make such mistakes. The circularity of his argument would consist not in its relation to any other position but rather in its relation to his own position.

VI

The Validity of Philosophical Arguments — II

In the last chapter, after coming to the conclusion that each of three critical philosophical arguments was addressed *ad hominem*, I argued that, in the absence of any *argumentum ad rem* in philosophy, all philosophical arguments are necessarily *ad hominem*. This argument immediately raises a question about its own status. I am claiming that it is a valid argument. This implies that it must itself be addressed *ad hominem*. How can this be?

By way of a reply, it is perhaps sufficient to point out that my argument does not, at least in any obvious way, miss the point of anyone who might contend that philosophical statements can be true or false independently of the arguments used to establish or disestablish them. It acquires its force precisely from the force of this contention; for the contention can only take the form of an argument, and this very argument will at once serve as a further illustration of the thesis that I have been advocating. Since it exposes the self-defeating character of what it attacks, my argument to the effect that all valid philosophical arguments are *ad hominem* — clearly itself a philosophical argument, and one that I am claiming is valid — is itself also *ad hominem*.

But it is clear that both my argument for the *ad hominem* character of valid philosophical arguments and my defense of the validity and the *ad hominem* character of this argument are disturbingly abstract. They invite the epithet "dialectical." Unfortunately, however, I know of no other argument for my general conclusion that is not at least equally abstract. Yet if I were content to rest my case on the three specific critical arguments that

I have discussed in detail, the result would be plainly inconclusive. A third mode of presentation, mediating the concrete and
the abstract, is required. This chapter will make use of such a
mode. It will consist in a classification of valid critical arguments
in philosophy. I shall not, however, discuss constructive philosophical arguments here, since they do not seem to me to differ
in interesting ways, and hence do not appear to be subject to any
fruitful classification. In addition, I believe, as I have already
explained, that critical arguments are more fundamental than
constructive ones.

It is important to insist at the outset that the only purpose of
the classification which I want to develop in this chapter is to
bridge the gap between concrete examples and an abstract generalization. If the result of classifying particular types of philosophical arguments according to the ways in which they are addressed *ad hominem* succeeds in suggesting that all types can be
classified according to these ways, I shall have accomplished my
entire objective. But the force of the classification is at most suggestive. To maintain that it is conclusive would be to beg the
question, since if some valid philosophical arguments are in fact
NOT *ad hominem,* it would be a *petitio* to claim that one has
classified them *all* according to the ways in which they ARE *ad
hominem.* Nor am I by any means claiming that my classification is the only one possible. Indeed, since mine is geared to a
particular and limited purpose, it is entirely arbitrary from any
point of view except the one that endorses just this purpose.

In discussing critical arguments that I regard as valid *argumenta ad hominem,* I have, in each case, availed myself of the
locution "defeats its own purpose." Indeed, an argument that
shows that a statement or argument defeats its own purpose is,
to my way of thinking, precisely an *argumentum ad hominem.*
A statement's *own* purpose, or an argument's *own* purpose could
only be a purpose of the maker of the statement or the user of
the argument; and the claim that the statement or argument in
question had *defeated* its own purpose could only mean that its
utterance or use was incompatible with such a purpose of its
maker or user. To *argue* that the statement or argument defeats
its own purpose is, then, to attempt to show that its maker or
user ought to admit the incompatibility. To argue *validly* is to

succeed in this attempt. But "purpose," as I am using the word at present, can clearly be construed as "principles of reasoning, . . . conduct, situation." For the purpose of a person making a philosophical statement or using a philosophical argument can only be to advocate principles of reasoning, conduct of a general sort, or acceptance of a certain general situation. Thus any argument that shows that a statement or argument defeats its own purpose establishes a conclusion concerning what a man ought to admit, in conformity with his principles of reasoning, or in consistency with his own conduct, situation, and so on. But this is almost a verbatim rendition of the definition of "argumentum ad hominem" supplied by Whately which I quoted in the last chapter. I could, in fact, have altogether avoided the irrelevant connotations of the phrase "argumentum ad hominem" in its ordinary usage by simply writing "argument showing that a statement or argument defeats its own purpose"; but the latter expression is so cumbersome that I preferred to take the risks associated with the former.

I have already mentioned that the classification of valid philosophical arguments that I want to develop reflects various ways in which such arguments can be *ad hominem*. It now appears that a way in which a valid philosophical argument can be *ad hominem* is a way in which it shows that a statement or argument defeats its own purpose. Now ways of showing that a statement or argument defeats its own purpose will differ according to the kinds of purpose involved. I should like to distinguish three senses of "purpose" in which a statement or argument may be said to have "defeated its own purpose." The first is a *general motive* capable of being shared by many people who make philosophical statements or use philosophical arguments, or by all such people. It is presumably a purpose, for instance, of all who state philosophical conclusions or argue for them, to engage in communication with other people. To adopt for the moment a Wittgensteinian *façon de parler:* it is not clear that there is any language-game except that of communication in which either stating or arguing is a legal move.

Communication is perhaps more a class of language-games than it is a specific game. A more nearly specific game would be that of communicating the literal truth. The intention to tell the

literal truth is a somewhat narrower general motive than is the
intention to communicate. People can make philosophical statements and use philosophical arguments without intending to tell
or reach the literal truth. They may seek to express themselves
but disclaim the relevance of standard criteria of truth and falsity
to such expression, as in the case of philosophers whose statements or arguments are fundamentally ironic or poetic. Communication is still the general motive of such philosophers. The
motive to tell or arrive at the truth is also general even if not
shared by the ironists and poets, because it is common to many
philosophical points of view.

A second sense of "purpose" is *specific motive.* By this, I
mean the ax that a philosopher has to grind in making the statements and using the arguments that he does. It is an interest in
defending the reliability of one or another mode of experience, or
in disabusing the world of a certain intellectual error. Empiricism, rationalism, pragmatism, nominalism, anti-intellectualism,
humanism, and opposition to assorted species of argument,
marked by the use of such labels as "The Megaric Fallacy," "The
Naturalistic Fallacy," and "The Fallacy of Simple Location," are
illustrations of philosophers' purposes at the level of specific motive.

The third sense of "purpose" to which the allegation that a
statement or argument defeats its own purpose may refer is the
content of the philosophical position that the statement or argument is intended, partially or fully, to express or support. For
it is surely a purpose of the person who makes the statement or
uses the argument to advocate what it expresses or supports. The
second and third versions of "purpose" may be illustrated by
pointing out that while the purpose of nominalism, in the sense
of *specific motive,* might be the desire to oppose the excesses of
platonism, its purpose as *content* would be advocacy of the view
that to be is to be an individual.

To criticize a philosophical statement or argument as having
defeated its own purpose is thus to impugn it in one of three
ways. It is to assert that acceptance of the statement or argument
would be incompatible with the fulfillment of the general or specific motive of its maker or user, or with the content of the position he is attempting to support by making or using it. Now such

incompatibility might be either *necessary* or *accidental*. It is necessary if implied by the content of the position. A general failure to communicate itself, for example, is inherent in the very *meaning* of any occultism; for such a view explicitly endorses the principle that the nature of the real cannot be communicated through discursive language. Thus whenever a position of this kind uses discursive language in the effort to make itself understood, it necessarily defeats its own purpose. In the case of some other position, however, the failure to communicate may not be unavoidable; it may just arise from an unfortunate but corrigible mode of expression. To point out such an infelicity is to engage in what might be called "an interrogative argument." For the force of the argument is only that of a demand for further clarification. On the other hand, to conclude that acceptance of a statement or argument made or used to advocate a position is necessarily incompatible with a purpose of the person who is advocating it, because implied by the content of the position, is to engage in a "destructive argument." Such an argument immediately indicts what it attacks.

The classification I have in mind is actually a cross-classification; it makes simultaneous use of both the distinction among three kinds of purpose and the distinction between accidental incompatibility and necessary incompatibility. I shall proceed at once to classify.

1. The first and broadest type of critical philosophical argument consists in pointing out that a philosopher whose general motive is to communicate has attempted to express or support his position by means of statements or arguments that are, in part or wholly, unintelligible. What is common to arguments of this type can be abstracted as "The Charge of Unintelligibility." Because an utterance might be unintelligible for one or another of several different reasons, there are at least four possible specifications of this charge: to wit, *tautology, occultness, ambiguity,* and *inconsistency*. It is obvious that the gravamen of the charge that a statement is tautologous is precisely that it has failed to communicate anything. Note that this charge would be pointless if it were not an *ad hominem* attack; for there is no *logical* objection to a tautology. Perhaps I have already said enough about the charge of occultness. Ambiguity and inconsistency can

be treated together. In communicating too much, the ambiguous or inconsistent statement or argument communicates nothing. That at least the charge of inconsistency is *ad hominem* was recognized by Joseph. "In the game of disputation," he said, "we may be held to score a victory if we force an opponent to an admission inconsistent with the thesis he propounded. But in the search for truth, to convict anyone of inconsistency is irrelevant; we have to determine what is true."[1] Much the same thing can be said about the situation in which an opponent is forced to admit that the statements crucial to the expression of his own position can be taken in several different senses.

Interrogative criticism, accusing a position of at least *prima facie* unintelligibility, has been a propaedeutic to more serious argumentation throughout the history of philosophy. Aristotle's examination of his predecessors and the technique of G. E. Moore come to mind. Destructive criticism based on this charge can also be documented copiously. The formula "Such-and-such a philosophical statement is either tautologous or false," perhaps first used as an explicit formula by the earlier British analysts but clearly an implicit principle of Plato's argumentation in the *Meno* and *Euthyphro,* shows that tautology and falsity have been regarded as equally glaring defects. Locke stigmatizes many statements about innate ideas as inherently occult. The charge of necessary ambiguity is often brought against a dualism that is systematically unable to draw a precise line between its allegedly independent principles. Necessary inconsistency has been found in just those dualisms that *do* draw a precise line; if mind and body are defined in such a way as to be independent of one another, then it is inconsistent to maintain that either can act on the other.

2. The philosopher whose general motive it is to tell the truth defeats his purpose if (a) he makes statements that by his own criteria of truth are false or if (b) he fails to indicate the evidence or argument that has led him to make the statements. Criticisms that focus upon such deficiencies can be classified under the heading of "The Charge of Dogmatism." Two specifications of this charge correspond respectively to (a) and (b) above.

---

1 H. W. B. Joseph, *An Introduction to Logic* (Oxford, Clarendon Press, 1916) p. 591, n. 2

(a) Very commonly, a philosopher who claims to be telling the truth attempts to support this claim by pointing to what
he calls evidence. Such a philosopher exposes himself to critical
argumentation based upon the principle that in philosophy what
lives by evidence must die by evidence. Argumentation over the
Teleological Argument exemplifies this point. The Teleological
Argument is sometimes referred to as an empirical argument
because one of its premises consists in the statement that the
Universe *is observed* to exhibit design. But the best way of re-
butting this argument is by inviting the man who uses it to take
another look at the Universe. For whatever type of design the
Universe has been observed to exhibit, it can also be observed
to lack. It may be tempting to think of this rebuttal as an exception to the rule that valid philosophical arguments are addressed *ad hominem*. But it would be an oversimplification to
suppose that the critic of the Teleological Argument is confining
himself to the facts. Indeed, the facts as such are of little interest
to him. What does interest him is only the use his opponent has
made of the facts. His rebuttal amounts to the insistence that he
be entitled to make the same use of facts that his opponent has
made. "If you can appeal to facts in establishing your thesis,
then I can appeal to facts to overthrow it," he is saying. Thus
what is *established* by this rebuttal is not that the Universe fails
to exhibit design, but that the man whose principles of reasoning
permit him to appeal to facts must be prepared to admit that the
facts cut both ways. The rebuttal, then, conforms exactly to the
definition of *"argumentum ad hominem"* that I have been assuming. The analysis of any other appeal to facts used in refuting
a philosophical argument or thesis would, I think, reveal a similar pattern. This pattern, furthermore, can obviously be fitted
into the broader pattern of argumentation to which the challenge
"Your statement is either tautologous or false" gives rise. For
when a philosopher is accused of having uttered a tautology, it
is usually clear enough to him that unless he can defend himself
against this accusation he has defeated his own purpose to communicate; and the defense very often takes the form of an appeal
to the facts, which his critic can also show to be self-defeating.

(b) A second specification of the Charge of Dogmatism
consists in criticizing a philosophical statement or argument not

on the ground that it is falsified by evidence of the very sort that it appeals to, but rather on the ground that its maker or user has failed to give a complete account of the evidence or principle of verification upon which it depends. For the claim to truth is unacceptable unless the possibility of verification exists. Where it is assumed, at least for the sake of the argument, that the defect is not necessarily inherent in the view under attack, the interrogative criticism that reveals it is simply a demand for the conditions under which the statement might be verified or the argument validated. Thinkers who regard a philosophical position as unacceptable unless it is based upon evidence — Bertrand Russell is an example — have used criticism of this kind with great success. Russell, in fact, is especially deft at using putatively interrogative argumentation of this sort for destructive purposes. When he asks whether there are any possible reasons for supposing that a certain statement is true, he usually manages to suggest that the statement is altogether indefensible. Part of the power of this suggestion derives from the insinuation that no statement could be defended at all except through an appeal to evidence of the sort that the critic himself regards as acceptable.

The refutation of philosophical "proofs" exemplifies interrogative criticism aiming to elicit the conditions under which the validity of an argument could be established. Those who attack the Ontological Proof or Mill's "Proof of the Principle of Utility" are seeking to demonstrate not the contradictory of the conclusion, but only the inadequacy of the argument to this conclusion. In effect, they are just asking for a better proof.

Destructive criticism aimed at dogmatism is akin to the attack upon occultness. For if the conditions of verification are *necessarily* elusive, then only the initiate can be said to perceive the truth of a statement under criticism. Indeed, this frequently is offered as the *definition* of the initiate. To point out that such occultness is self-defeating is a polemical device of long standing. More generally, pragmatism and logical positivism have been much concerned, if not entirely preoccupied, with what they have taken to be the inherent incapacity of transcendentalisms to supply the conditions of their own verification. The Verifiability Principle has in our day become one of the most familiar ways of attacking an alien point of view.

3. Communication and truth are among the *general* motives behind the use of a philosophical statement or argument. I turn now to "purpose" in the sense of *"specific* motive," and to the ways in which purposes, so construed, might be self-defeating. One such purpose might be the specific motive to condemn a certain kind of error. A position dedicated to a purpose of this kind would defeat its own purpose if it chanced to commit the same error it aimed to abolish. The exposure of such an error in the position under attack may be identified as "The Charge of *Tu Quoque.*" An example of this sort of argument is the statement that Whitehead, who opposed "the bifurcation of nature," bifurcated nature himself.[2] More recently, critics of Gilbert Ryle, who exposed "category mistakes" in *The Concept of Mind,* have gleefully accused Ryle of committing "category mistakes" in the same book.

Tu Quoque is a distinctive type of criticism only if it is not argued that the error to which it calls attention is necessary to the philosophy under attack. Thus it operates only as invitation to revise and clarify. It is often held, of course, that a position *necessarily* commits an error of which it accuses others. But the various ways in which such a view might defeat its own purpose are better considered under some of the following rubrics than here. I shall assume that the Charge of *Tu Quoque* appears in interrogative criticism only.

4. Whatever the specific motive for proposing a philosophical position may be, there is always the possibility that the statements or arguments through which the position is expressed do not do justice to that motive. If not, this is a further sort of incompatibility between a philosophy and its purpose. Aristotle exposes such an incompatibility when he points out that Plato's doctrine of Ideas, proposed in the effort to explain sensible existence, is inherently incapable of explaining sensible existence. Thus the doctrine of Ideas is an altogether ineffective way of satisfying the motive that it was intended to satisfy. This type of criticism may be called "The Charge of Ineffectiveness." As in the first two rubrics, there is a distinction between accidental and

---

[2] H. K. Wells, *Process and Unreality* (New York, King's Crown Press, 1950); cited by A. H. Johnson in "Recent Discussions of Alfred North Whitehead," *The Review of Metaphysics,* Vol. 5, 1951, pp. 293-308

necessary defect. To point to the former is never more than to demand further elaboration, while to call attention to the latter is to impeach the position in question without further inquiry. There are many brilliant examples of polemic asserting the essential incompatibility of a position's specific motives with the statements or arguments that constitute the development of the position. One is Bradley's attack on all outlooks that regard the maintenance of the reality of the self as an ultimate desideratum.[3] Another is Locke's attack on the supposition that innate ideas are required to explain the distinction between propositions universally assented to and those not receiving such assent.[4] In general, this is the type of criticism that exploits cases of "throwing out the baby with the bath" or of "proving too much." Both Aristotle's argument against Eudoxus and Berkeley's against the "materialists" seem also to belong here. Eudoxus' argument, according to Aristotle, is a necessarily ineffective way of showing that pleasure is the chief good; and the argument of the "materialists," on Berkeley's showing, necessarily fails to establish the need for material substance.

5. A further method of criticism consists in objecting that a philosophical position presupposes exactly what certain statements or arguments through which the position is articulated deny. Thus, it may be argued, the statement, "Life is a dream," is meaningful only if dreams are distinguishable from waking-life. This distinction is therefore presupposed by the position on behalf of which the statement is made. But the statement itself amounts to a denial of the possibility of making the distinction. Other examples are the refutation of "Man is fundamentally selfish"[5] and of "All men are hypocrites."[6] All these may be subsumed under the heading "The Charge of Denying Presuppositions." Lest it be thought that this Charge can be applied only to reductionisms, it is worth noting that Aristotle applies it to Plato's doctrine of Ideas, saying that "the arguments for the Ideas

---

[3] *Appearance and Reality* (London, Swan Sonnenschein & Co., 1897) Ch. X

[4] *An Essay Concerning Human Understanding*, Bk. I, Ch. II, Secs. 17-19

[5] David Hume, *An Inquiry Concerning the Principles of Morals*, Appendix II

[6] Gilbert Ryle, *The Concept of Mind* (London, Hutchinson's University Library, 1949) pp. 172-174

destroy the very principles on which those who believe in the Ideas rely much more than they rely even on Ideas."[7] Criticism that makes this Charge is always destructive rather than interrogative, because it refers to the content of a position under attack rather than just to general or specific motives behind the assertion of the position.

6. A philosophical position defeats its own purpose when that purpose is to advocate a content whose successful advocacy could not, by its own account, be genuine knowledge. Traditional empiricism, for example, which defines knowledge as a product of sense-perception, has often been criticized for a systematic incapacity to show its own origin in sense-perception. The third of the critical arguments that I analyzed in Chapter V made a similar point about naturalism. Other statements and arguments that have been attacked by well-known versions of this type of criticism are ones in favor of skepticism, positivism, behaviorism, pragmatism, intuitionism, and the coherence theory. The type of criticism itself may be called "The Charge of Self-Disqualification." It is distinguished from the Charge of Denying Presuppositions in that what it brings to bear against the statement or argument criticized is a consideration explicitly endorsed by the position being put forward, whereas the latter merely points out that the position *presupposes* what the statement or argument denies.

A somewhat disguised form of the Charge of Self-Disqualification is the attempt to derive or explain the position of one's opponent. Thus Mill states that only a moralist having utilitarian motives could be a Kantian.[8] This attack will not be effective unless the "Kantian" to whom it is addressed accepts the principles of Utilitarianism. On the face of it, this seems unlikely. But to the extent that such a refutation is successful, it succeeds by showing that a position is intelligible only on grounds alien to it; and this is the common basis of all criticism aiming to exhibit Self-Disqualification.

---

[7] *Metaphysics*, 1079a 14-16, Hope translation (New York, Columbia University Press, 1952)

[8] "Utilitarianism," Everyman's Edition, pp. 3-4. For a generalization of this polemic, see Jeremy Bentham, *An Introduction to the Principles of Morals and Legislation*, Ch. I, Sect. 13-14. Attacks of this sort are also frequently made by pragmatists; e.g., Dewey.

7. There are, finally, philosophies that may be attacked for denying their own existence. Nominalism, for example, has traditionally faced this criticism, for in an extreme form it would seem to reduce to the proposition that there are no propositions. I shall identify this type of criticism as "The Charge of Self-Denial."[9]

In the order in which I have given it, this series of types may be correlated with a series of philosophical positions ranging from reductionistic to rationalistic. The polemic of a "scientific" or "tough-minded" philosophy consists largely in criticizing less reductionistic views for a failure to communicate themselves. Corresponding to the Charge of Dogmatism, there is also likely to be an emphasis on verifiability, as in pragmatism and logical positivism. But methods such as those of Self-Disqualification and Self-Denial will be looked on as mere dialectical tricks, to be discounted as jejune and a priori.

More conservative philosophies, such as realism in both its traditional and its more recent form, gravitate polemically toward the center of the series. No position is rejected out of hand as unintelligible; a genuine effort is made to understand all points of view. And once understood, alien positions are repudiated not as merely dogmatic, but as answerable to the Charges of *Tu Quoque* and Ineffectiveness. Some realists have expressed an interest in the polemic of Self-Disqualification and Self-Denial; but on the whole realism distrusts the notion of a "necessarily defective" view, and prefers interrogative to destructive polemic.

Positions that see no reason to be dissatisfied with "the high priori" concentrate on the types of criticism occurring last in my series. It would be typical of both Critical and Objective Idealism to make liberal use of the Charges of Denying Presuppositions and Self-Disqualification, especially in attacking reductionisms. Criticisms based on Ineffectiveness might also occur, but only necessary ineffectiveness would be likely to be attacked. For a view of this sort will avow that it aims to concern itself with genuine philosophies only, not corrigible slips of the tongue.

---

9 I owe the distinction between what I have called Self-Disqualification and Self-Denial to Ledger Wood's suggestion in *The Analysis of Knowledge* (Princeton University Press, 1941) pp. 194-199, to the effect that "There are no propositions" must be treated on a wholly different footing from "There are no truths." For, as Wood points out, "The denial of truth is not itself a truth as the denial of propositions is a proposition." (p. 199)

VII

Hume's Argument
Concerning Causal Necessity

One difference between an argument and a dogmatic statement in philosophy is that unless one's interlocutor already believes the dogma, he can always waive it in favor of another
better to his liking; whereas, to the extent that an argument is
effective, it cannot be waived. But the difference is partly one of
degree; many arguments are based upon assumptions that can be
waived to the extent that they are dogmas. An ideally effective
argument would be one based upon an assumption that one's
opponent cannot waive, in view of the fact that he cannot regard
it as a dogma alien to his own beliefs. An argument of this sort
would radically contrast, however, with the mere endorsement
of an opponent's dogma; it would take that dogma seriously only
in order to exhibit it as subverting itself. I have referred to this
type of argument as a valid species of *argumentum ad hominem*.
In an argument of this sort, the arguer proceeds by making,
merely for the sake of the argument, an assumption necessary to
his opponent's point of view, and shows that this assumption has
consequences both embarrassing to the opponent and unsuspect-
ed by him, in the sense that they lie beyond the portion of his
doctrine which he has as yet thought out.

Argumentum ad hominem is the philosopher's basic weapon
of attack. His standard defense consists in disarming anyone who
attempts to argue *ad hominem* against his position. What he
must do is to show that the opposition has not taken his position

seriously enough — that the attack has, in effect, offered only a
dogma in return for a dogma. What is involved here is an inverse
of *argumentum ad hominem.* Instead of endorsing the presuppositions of one's interlocutor with the intent of exploiting them,
one shows that the latter has failed to endorse one's own presuppositions and thus is entitled to no exploitation of them. He
has assumed precisely what one is denying, or has denied precisely what one is assuming. It is a temptation to refer to this
type of argument as *"argumentum ab homine,"* on the analogy
of *"argumentum ad hominem."* In standard usage, however, a
phrase such as "accusing one's opponent of *petitio principii"*
would be employed, and I want to avoid the proliferation of
terminology. But it is necessary to remark that by *"petitio principii"* I shall never mean circularity of proof, definition, or argument. A few chapters back, I asserted that Mill's "Proof of the
Principle of Utility" is circular. I would not want to say, however,
that Mill commits a *petitio* in this argument. For he does not
assert anything here that his opponents have explicitly denied,
or deny anything that they have explicitly asserted. On the other
hand, those who reject Mill's "Proof" on the ground that "capable
of being desired" is not synonymous with "worthy of being desired" do commit a *petitio,* for they are denying an explicit principle of Utilitarianism, and their denial, undefended as it is, is no
more than a dogmatic pronouncement. I shall have more to say
about circular definitions and proofs as this chapter progresses.

I want to attempt now to document these general observations in terms of some of Hume's arguments about the necessity
of cause. I choose these arguments because of their great famili-
arity and historical significance; it is of crucial importance to any
theory of philosophical argumentation that it give a plausible account of them. In particular, my purpose will be to show how
my generalizations may be used to classify the various arguments
of Hume as relatively effective or ineffective. To this end it is
necessary to disregard the order in which Hume himself presents
them, and even to overlook the distinction between arguments
opposing the Principle of Causality (that whatever begins to
exist must necessarily have a cause) and those opposing the
Principle of Causation (that particular causes must necessarily
have the same particular effects). Such matters are no doubt

essential to the study of Hume's metaphysical or epistemological conclusions as such. But I shall be interested only in the argumentative methods through which conclusions of this sort are secured.

1. The arguments that I should like to discuss first are those that seem to me to be the most effective; to wit, those that lie nearest to the polar ideals of *argumentum ad hominem* and the fully justified charge of *petitio.* The latter is adequately illustrated by a well-known argument.

> Every thing, 'tis said, must have a cause; for if any thing wanted a cause, *it* wou'd produce *itself;* that is, exist before it existed; which is impossible. But this reasoning is plainly inconclusive; because it supposes, that in our denial of a cause we still grant what we expressly deny, *viz.,* that there must be a cause; which therefore is taken to be the object itself . . . . [But to exclude] all external causes, excludes *a fortiori* the thing itself which is created. An object, that exists absolutely without any cause, certainly is not its own cause.[1]

The situation occasioning this rejoinder is one in which Hume's opponent (namely, Samuel Clarke) has attempted to extract from a position like Hume's own the absurdity that an object might be its own cause. But the effect of the rejoinder is to show that the true significance of this position has escaped its attacker, who has therefore failed in his effort to exploit it. Any further commentary on this argument seems gratuitous; its force is obvious.

2. The opposite pole of *argumentum ad hominem* is exemplified by the following passage. Since the point of this argument is not so immediately clear as that of the preceding example, it is necessary to reproduce Hume's text in some detail, and then to make a few comments.

> The *Cartesians* . . . , having establish'd it as a principle, that we are perfectly acquainted with the essence of matter, have very naturally inferr'd, that it is endow'd with no efficacy, and that 'tis impossible for it of itself to communicate motion, or to produce any of those effects, which we ascribe to it. As the essence of matter consists in extension, and as extension implies not actual motion, but only mobility; they conclude, that the energy, which produces the motion, cannot lie in the extension.

---

[1] *A Treatise of Human Nature,* ed. by L. A. Selby-Bigge (Oxford, Clarendon Press, 1888) pp. 80-81. In the present chapter, all references to the Treatise will refer in particular to this edition.

> This conclusion leads them to another. . . . Matter, say they, is
> in itself entirely unactive, and depriv'd of any power, by which
> it may produce, or continue, or communicate motion: But since
> these effects are evident to our senses, and since the power, that
> produces them, must be placed somewhere, it must lie in the
> DEITY . . . .
>
> . . . Now as . . . instances [of power and efficacy] can never be
> discover'd in body, the *Cartesians,* proceeding upon their princi-
> ple of innate ideas, have had recourse to a supreme spirit or
> deity, whom they consider as . . . the immediate cause of every
> alteration in matter. But the principle of innate ideas being al-
> low'd to be false, it follows, that the supposition of a deity can
> serve us in no stead, in accounting for [the] idea of agency. . . .
> Since these philosophers, therefore, have concluded, that matter
> cannot be endow'd with any efficacious principle, because 'tis
> impossible to discover in it such a principle; the same course of
> reasoning shou'd determine them to exclude it from the supreme
> being.[2]

Before discussing the force of this argument, it is necessary
to note that one of the points involved in Hume's statement of
it not only is irrelevant but would vitiate the argument if it were
relevant. The irrelevant point is the outright repudiation of innate ideas. This could, of course, have absolutely no appeal for
a Cartesian, for whom innate ideas are fundamental. Not that
innate ideas are incapable of being effectively attacked. Locke's
polemic against them is as clear-cut an example of influential
argumentation as is Hume's entire discussion of causal necessity.
But no doctrine can be convincingly attacked merely by denying
it; and in the present instance this is all that Hume does.

The main theme of this argument does, however, exhibit
great force. This theme may be paraphrased as follows.

> The Cartesians have asserted that matter possesses no power, be-
> cause they discover none in it. But since they also affirm that
> the effects of power are evident to our senses, they feel that the
> source of these effects must be located somewhere; and so they
> ascribe power to God. But the same principle that led them to
> deny that matter possesses power should also have led them
> to deny that God can possess it.

This argument is effective because, to the extent that Hume's
antagonist (namely, Malebranche) actually takes the position
depicted by Hume, he must, if he is honest with himself, come to
conclusions which undercut the very assumption that power exists. As Reid remarked in commenting upon Hume's criticisms

---

[2] *Ibid.,* pp. 159-160

of the Cartesians, "Des Cartes' system of the human understanding . . . hath some original defect; . . . this scepticism is inlaid in it and reared along with it."[3] In exposing the skepticism latent in the presuppositions of anyone defending this version of Cartesianism, Hume's argument is clearly *ad hominem* in the sense defined above.

3. Sometimes it is unnecessary to distinguish between *argumentum ad hominem* and the charge of *petitio*. Cases of this sort occur where Hume argues in such a way that it is a matter of indifference whether the viewpoint whose consequences he is seeking to elicit is his own or that of his rivals. Such a situation is involved in the following passage.

> All the points of time and place, say some philosophers, in which we can suppose any object to begin to exist, are in themselves equal; and unless there is some cause, which is peculiar to one time and to one place, . . . it must remain in eternal suspence; and the object can never begin to be, for want of something to fix its beginning. But I ask; is there any more difficulty in supposing the time and place to be fix'd without a cause, than to suppose the existence to be determined in that manner?[4]

The question here is whether it is Hume himself, or the philosopher he opposes (namely, Hobbes), who is supposed to have no more difficulty in conceiving the time and place to be fixed without a cause than in conceiving existence to be causeless. If it is Hume himself, then he is accusing his antagonist of underestimating the scope of what he, Hume, on his own assumptions, is capable of conceiving, so that the attack upon Hume's doctrine, based as it is upon this underestimation, turns out to be abortive. On this interpretation, the argument is a charge of *petitio*. If, on the other hand, it is Hume's antagonist who is alleged to be capable of conceiving the time and place of an object fixed without a cause, then this capacity must arise directly from what that antagonist assumes; viz., that he can conceive the existence of an object to be determined without a cause. In this case, the argument exploits only the position of Hume's antagonist, and therefore is an *argumentum ad hominem*. On either alternative, it operates with constraining force.

---

[3] *An Inquiry into the Human Mind on the Principles of Common Sense*, Ch. I, Sect. VII

[4] *Treatise*, p. 80

4. Another argument presenting this duality is the afterthought to the *Treatise* which becomes the fulcrum of Hume's examination of necessary connection in the *Enquiry*.

> Some have asserted, that we feel an energy, or power, in our own mind; and that having in this manner acquir'd the idea of power, we transfer that quality to matter, where we are not able immediately to discover it. . . . But to convince us how fallacious this reasoning is, we need only consider, that the will being here consider'd as a cause, has no more a discoverable connexion with its effects, than any material cause has with its proper effect. So far from perceiving the connexion betwixt an act of volition, and a motion of the body; 'tis allow'd that no effect is more inexplicable from the powers and essence of thought and matter.[5]

If the crux of this argument is the proposition that Hume's principles permit him to find no more satisfaction in internal than in external energy, then the opponent who has arbitrarily distinguished between them has begged the question. But if the argument hinges rather on the proposition that the *opponent's* principles, on which the latter has already abandoned external energy, require him also to abandon internal energy, then it is addressed *ad hominem*. The text does not reveal which of these options Hume has in mind. But since the choice between them may be expressed as the minor premise of a dilemma, this is entirely an academic question.

By no means all of Hume's arguments, however, are as cogent as the ones just cited. I turn now to some of those that seem to me to be less than maximally effective.

5. One difference between *petitio principii*, in the sense in which I am using the term here, and circularity is that in order to show that a philosopher's argument or definition is viciously or benignly circular one need not prove that he has failed to take one's own point of view seriously. This contrast is illustrated by the following argument.

> Shou'd any one . . . pretend to define a cause, by saying it is something productive of another, 'tis evident he wou'd say nothing. For what does he mean by *production*? Can he give any definition of it, that will not be the same with that of causation? . . . If he cannot; he here runs in a circle, and gives a synonimous term instead of a definition.[6]

---

[5] *Ibid.,* p. 632. Cf. also pp. 90-91, 157; and *Hume's Enquiries,* ed. by L. A. Selby-Bigge (Oxford, Clarendon Press, 1894) pp. 64-69

[6] *Treatise,* p. 77

Here Hume does not call attention in any way to his own doctrine. It might be supposed that his neutrality would make for a stronger argument than one based upon considerations not neutral to his own doctrine, such as any of the charges of *petitio* cited above. But the reverse is true. For the argument just quoted could be waived by any opponent who genuinely believed "production" to be prior in definition to "cause." In general, the charge of circularity in definition is rarely effective in philosophical disputes, precisely because the order in which terms are defined is relative to the outlook in which they occur. What philosophical terms are to be regarded as synonymous is itself a philosophical question.[7] Unlike the first four cited, then, this is one of Hume's least effective rebuttals.

6. Many of Hume's arguments regarding cause attack theories considered merely as possible solutions of a given problem, and so do not suggest that Hume had in mind any actual opponent. But so long as these theories are specific philosophical positions, it is a matter of indifference for the present analysis whether or not they were, in fact, maintained by anyone; all that I am now attempting to ascertain is the effectiveness of the arguments against these positions as stated. A case in point is a well-known argument in which Hume accuses a possible opponent of circularity in *proof;* this contrasts with the last quotation from Hume, since that charged the opposition with circularity in *definition.*

> Let us consider all the arguments, upon which [the] proposition [that instances, of which we have had no experience, must resemble those, of which we have had experience] may be suppos'd to be founded, and as these must be deriv'd either from *knowl-*

---

[7] A further ground on which Hume's argument may be waived is expressed by Reid:

"Surely [Hume] was not ignorant that there are many things of which we have a clear and distinct conception, which are so simple in their nature that they cannot be defined any other way than by synonymous words.

"He might here have applied to *power* and *efficacy,* what he says, in another place, of *pride* and *humility.* 'The passions of *pride* and *humility,*' he says, 'being simple and uniform impressions, it is impossible we can ever give a just definition of them. As the words are of general use, and the things they represent the most common of any, every one, of himself, will be able to form a just notion of them without danger of mistake.'" (*Essays on the Active Powers of Man,* Ch. III)

edge or *probability,* let us cast our eyes on each of these degrees
of evidence, and see whether they afford any just conclusion of
this nature.

❋   ❋   ❋   ❋   ❋

Probability . . . must in some respects be founded on the impressions of our memory and senses, and in some respects on our
ideas. Were there no mixture of any impression in our probable
reasonings, the conclusion wou'd be entirely chimerical: And
were there no mixture of ideas, the action of the mind, in observing the relation, wou'd, properly speaking, be sensation, not
reasoning . . . .
The only connexion or relation of objects, which can lead us beyond the immediate impressions of our memory and senses, is
that of cause and effect. . . . The idea of cause and effect is
deriv'd from *experience,* which informs us, that such particular
objects, in all past instances, have been constantly conjoin'd with
each other: And as an object similar to one of these is suppos'd
to be immediately present in its impression, we thence presume
on the existence of one similar to its usual attendant. According
to this account of things, . . . probability is founded on the presumption of a resemblance betwixt those objects, of which we
have had experience, and those of which we have had none; and
therefore 'tis impossible this presumption can arise from probability. The same principle cannot be both cause and effect of
another. [8]

Thus it is circular to suppose that the uniformity of nature
is probable, when probability itself is based upon the presumption of that uniformity. It is circular, that is, on Hume's assumptions; but it is not necessarily circular from every point of view.
Hume carefully states his own assumptions during the course of
the argument; chief among these is the supposition that our
knowledge of probabilities is derived wholly from experience.
And in the last sentence quoted above he very nearly suggests
a point of view on which this supposition would be gratuitous.
For what does Hume have in mind when he refers to the uniformity of nature as the *cause* of probability? Only that the
former produces the latter, being ontologically prior to it. And
what is his intention in characterizing this uniformity as the
effect of probability? All that he can mean is that the former is
known through the latter, which thus has epistemological priority
over it. Now there are obviously positions that distinguish between ontological and epistemological priority, and which there-

---

[8] *Treatise,* pp. 89-90; cf. *Enquiry,* pp. 36-38

fore would need only to make this distinction explicit in order to answer the charge that "*p* because *q* and *q* because *p*" is circular. In particular, a realistic or "a priori" theory of induction could waive this entire argument, contending that it represents only a *petitio* on Hume's part. The argument is, of course, binding upon Hume's point of view, for if all knowledge of probabilities is derived from experience, then there is no epistemological channel leading to a transempirical uniformity productive of our experience of probability; and as a result there will be no genuine ontological order to be distinguished from epistemological order. All of this shows that whether a given proof in philosophy is circular depends upon the outlook in which it occurs, just as no philosophical definition is circular except in relation to a specific defining position. I think it must be concluded that since Hume misses this point in the argument now under consideration, the latter has serious limitations.

7. Now I should like to consider those of Hume's arguments regarding causal necessity that hinge directly upon what many of his commentators have referred to as his "dogmas." The dogmas involved in this aspect of Hume's doctrine are the so-called "copy theory" of ideas ("That all our simple ideas . . . are deriv'd from simple impressions, which are correspondent to them, and which they exactly represent"[9]) and the proposition that whatever is distinguishable is separable. A third undefended assumption, that "relations of ideas" and "matters of fact" are exclusive and exhaustive, plays a part in Hume's argumentation, not as a premise but only as a methodological device that serves to establish the alternatives to be considered at each stage of the inquiry into the origins of the ideas associated with cause. No one argument depends upon this last assumption.

One cannot be altogether confident in discussing the function of the copy theory in Hume's arguments concerning cause. The significance Hume attaches to it is suggested by his statement that " 'tis impossible perfectly to understand any idea, without tracing it up to its origin, and examining that primary impression, from which it arises."[10] The difficulty is to ascertain whether in

---

[9] *Treatise*, p. 4
[10] *Ibid.*, pp. 74-75

this case he was seeking merely to explicate an idea whose genuineness he never questioned, or whether he supposed that to understand this idea would be to see it as an illusion. Certainly his initial datum is at least the appearance of an idea of causal necessity. If he supposed the idea to be genuine, then one may think of his entire treatment of causal necessity as a quest for its origin. In this case, the copy theory operates primarily as a methodological principle; it governs his attempt "perfectly to understand" the idea. Sometimes, it is true, Hume's rejection of a supposititious component of the idea — for example, "force" — seems to be dictated by a direct application of the copy theory: Hume can find in his experience no corresponding impression. Yet in such cases this application does not in itself constitute an argument; rather, it raises suspicions strongly suggesting that a certain position is vulnerable to criticism. Thus the copy theory is not itself a premise of any argument.

It is possible, on the other hand, that Hume supposed that the idea of cause was spurious — an initial datum, perhaps, but not a trustworthy conclusion. In this case, his discussion of causal necessity may be regarded as a sort of inductive support for the copy theory itself. According to the latter, the absence of any impression of cause as such implies the absence of any idea of it. Therefore, each candidate for the role of this idea must be disqualified: logical necessity, force, volitional energy, and so on. Each candidate, moreover, must be disqualified in its own terms; for, as Hume knew, to argue against any candidate merely on the ground that a correspondent impression is lacking would be to assume the truth of the copy theory and thus to argue in a circle. On the present hypothesis, then, as on the former and more probable one, no argument involves the copy theory as a premise; so it is irrelevant to the purposes of this chapter to consider it further.

This brings us to the arguments in which Hume assumes the dogma that "Whatever is distinguishable is separable." Perhaps the clearest example of these is the following:

> We can never demonstrate the necessity of a cause to every new existence, or new modification of existence, without shewing at the same time the impossibility there is, that any thing can ever begin to exist without some productive principle . . . . [But] as all distinct ideas are separable from each other, and as the ideas

> of cause and effect are evidently distinct, 'twill be easy for us
> to conceive any object to be non-existent this moment, and exist-
> ent the next, without conjoining to it the distinct idea of a cause
> or productive principle.[11]

This passage is also clearly illustrative of the flaw which is common to all the arguments based upon the same assumption. This is the *petitio* that Hume commits in supposing cause and effect to be sharply distinct. It is a *petitio* because the rationalists whom Hume is attacking would regard the distinction between cause and effect as less than ultimately real; both cause and effect, on this view, are merely temporal aspects of a nontemporal unity. The proposition that whatever is conceivable is possible, which for Hume is a corollary of "whatever is distinguishable is separable," is open to objections of the same kind. For the question at issue is only "What is conceivable?" and what is conceivable to Hume would be inconceivable to his rationalistic opponents. Leibniz, for example, would surely have been shocked by the statement that we can form "a clear and consistent idea of one body's moving upon another, and of its rest immediately upon the contact; or of its returning back in the same line, in which it came; or of its annihilation; or circular or elliptical motion; and in short, of an infinite number of other changes, which we may suppose it to undergo."[12]

8. All that now remains is to comment upon the extent to which Hume's psychological conclusions concerning the idea of necessary connection constitute a further argument against causal necessity. It is a powerful rhetorical device to supplement an attack on an opponent's view with an explanation of the origins of that view in terms of motives or causes extrinsic to its truth. A proposal may be exhibited not only as worthless in itself, but also as arising from the understandable naïveté or private interest of its proponent. This seems to be at least a part of Hume's intent in exhibiting the idea of necessary connection as the product of habit or custom.

This device, however, is dialectically efficacious, rather than merely rhetorically persuasive, only when the person against whom it is addressed must necessarily admit the proposed ex-

---

[11] *Ibid.,* p. 79. Cf. *Enquiry,* p. 35
[12] *Treatise,* p. 111

planation of his view. In such a case the argument is one of the most powerful types of *argumentum ad hominem* — a type that I have already classified as the Charge of Self-Disqualification. An example would be the explanation, on naturalistic grounds, of the advocacy of naturalism. But it is clear that Hume's account of the source of the idea of necessary connection would fail to have this force. For there is no discernible reason why any of his opponents would, on their own principles, have been constrained to accept his psychology.

Most studies of Hume's discussion of cause have been primarily motivated by the desire to elicit evidence toward a coherent statement of his ultimate epistemological or metaphysical conclusions. In this chapter, I have not taken issue with that motivation. Instead, I have tried to suggest an entirely independent and apparently novel mode of analysis. There would seem to be no reason why analysis of this sort could not be applied to Hume's arguments in other areas, as well as to the arguments of other philosophers. The examination of arguments is, at a minimum, a significant adjunct to the examination of conclusions. For unless the relevant arguments are taken into account, it is difficult to see why one conclusion ought to be adopted rather than any other.

VIII

Formal Systems and Ontological Systems

In this chapter I want to concern myself directly with the question I raised in the Introduction as to whether the relations among opposing philosophical positions are fundamentally logical relations. The only properties of philosophical positions that seem relevant to this investigation are properties that belong to a philosophical position by virtue of its role as an "ontological system." The conclusions I wish to advocate with regard to the oppositions among ontological systems are best reached in terms of a comparison of such systems with what are called "formal systems."

Since this is not primarily a technical study, there is no reason why I should add one more entry to the list of technical definitions of "formal system" that have been contributed in recent years. For my purposes, it will suffice to consider briefly a fragment of a sample formal system that illustrates some of the properties that I shall have in mind in speaking of formal systems in general. Suppose, then, that someone were to notice the following things about the relationships among selected points on a line:

(1) If point a is to the right of point b, then point b is not to the right of point a;

(2) No point is to the right of itself;

(3) If point a is to the right of point b, and point b is to the right of point c, then point a is to the right of point c;

and so on.

The person who made these observations, or someone else, might notice that the three statements are not altogether unrelated. In particular, if we permit a certain sort of logical inference, then (2) follows from (1). For if a be substituted for b in (1) we have

(4) If point a is to the right of point a, then point a is not to the right of point a.

Now if we decide to use the principle of *reductio ad absurdum* — that is, the principle that any proposition that implies its own denial is false — then we can infer from (4) that since "Point a is to the right of point a" implies its own denial, it must be false that point a is to the right of point a. Since "point a" here refers to any point whatsoever, this last statement simply means "No point is to the right of itself," which is just (2) again. The relationship between (1) and (2) can now be expressed by saying that (1) is a *postulate* and (2) a *theorem*. Not enough information has yet been given to enable anyone to decide whether (3) is a postulate or a theorem. But it cannot be both. Any one formal system is a class of statements having at least two distinct subclasses, which are called "postulates" and "theorems." (In many commonly studied formal systems, these two subclasses exhaust the statements belonging to the system as well as excluding each other.) Of course, there may be some other formal system in which both (1) and (2) appear, but in which either (1) is not a postulate or (2) is not a theorem. A formal system is determined partly by the class of statements selected as its postulates. Another determining factor is the set of logical principles — deductive schemata — that can be legitimately used to infer theorems from postulates. Many such "rules of inference" are common to most formal systems; there are very few systems, for example, that do not permit the use of *modus ponens*. On the other hand, the principle of *reductio ad absurdum*, required in order to infer (2) from (1) in the present system, is by no means common. There are many systems in which its use is not authorized.

I have spoken of factors that determine a formal system. Someone who examines further the fragment of a system that I have discussed may notice that one thing that does *not* determine *this* system is its specific content. Neither the membership of the class of theorems nor the logical structure of the proofs that establish this membership has anything at all to do with the fact that the system is concerned with the relation "is to the right of" as such. It could equally well have been concerned with "is to the left of," "is greater than," or "is stronger than." Of course, it would not have done justice to the relation "is equal to" or "is the successor of."

I turn now to the idea of "an ontological system." Unfortunately, I cannot do much by way of specifying this idea in advance. It will, I hope, receive clarification throughout this chapter. As a first approximation, what I have in mind when I use the phrase "ontological system" is the systematic context of any statement of the form "To be is . . . ." Examples of such statements are: "To be is to be perceived," "To be is to be an individual," "To be is to be intelligible," "To be is to be a whole," "To be is to be a material object," and so on. Obviously, these statements have systematic contexts; they are not uttered as offhand remarks.

One way to begin attempting to establish real differences between ontological systems and formal systems is simply to point to differences that appear at a *prima facie* level. For example, when the grounds of a statement within a formal system are demanded, that demand can be satisfied merely by exhibiting the postulates of the system that imply the statement in question. But when the grounds of an ontological statement are demanded, the demand is never satisfied by exhibiting ontological "postulates," since these "postulates" themselves at once become the locus of the issue, rather than the "theorems" that they are alleged to support. I have already referred to this phenomenon in Chapter V.[1] Certain versions of the Teleological Argument for the existence of God come to mind as further examples of it. The premise that the Universe exhibits design is certainly no less open to criticism than is the conclusion it is alleged to support. Issues may, of course, arise with respect to the truth of the postu-

---

[1] See pp. 58, 68, 76

lates of formal systems, but such issues are not relevant to the evaluation of formal systems insofar as they are formal. The issues that arise with respect to the truth of the "postulates" of ontological systems are, on the other hand, directly relevant to the evaluation of the systems themselves. Another way of making the distinction I have in mind is to say that ontological systems cannot be divided into the two (or more) exclusive classes of statements comprising formal systems; for the very distinction between postulates and theorems is not quite tenable in an ontological system.

Another difference between ontological and formal systems is that when an ontological system is impugned as inconsistent, ambiguous, or question-begging, it can usually be reformulated in such a way as to meet the criticisms in question, although the new version will likely be subject to further criticisms of a similar nature. On a number of occasions, fatal logical flaws have been found in the Ontological Argument for the existence of God. Those who would like to use this argument, however, have never found it difficult to present a new and improved version, free at least of the defects in question. Thus the logical credit of the system that includes, and to some extent depends upon, the Ontological Argument was, temporarily at any rate, restored. A defective formal system, however, cannot properly be said to lend itself to any reformulation that overcomes its defects. For a formal system can be reformulated only as an equivalent system, and a system free of defects could not be equivalent to a defective one. It would be more accurate to say that a defective system is *replaced* by a new system without the defects of the former. In any event, the discovery of flaws of a purely logical nature represents a much more serious indictment of a formal system than of an ontological one. The proponent of a logically defective formal system usually acknowledges an obligation to withdraw the system once the defects have been brought to light, while the advocate of a logically defective ontological system seldom acknowledges any such obligation.

A third difference, related to the first two, also deserves attention. One important purpose of a formal system is fulfilled when proofs for the statements of technical interest that belong to the system but are not postulates have been constructed. The question whether a proven statement is true or false is irrelevant to this purpose of the system. The question of the truth or falsity of an ontological statement may arise, however, regardless of how it is related to others in the system to which it belongs. The purpose of the system is not to prove any such statement, at least in the strict sense of "prove." It is just to show that it is true. The distinction between truth and proof does not have the same function in the critique of ontological systems that it does in the critique of formal systems.

Yet while the question whether particular statements and classes of statements occurring in formal systems have been proved or can be proved can be sharply distinguished from the question whether they are true, the *notion* of proof in formal systems cannot be elucidated without an at least implicit appeal to the notion of truth. For genuine proof is possible only within a consistent system, and the consistency of a system can be established only by showing that it has a model. Truth, then, enters the picture as the correspondence between the statements of the system and the properties of any one of its models.

Because of its bearing upon the differences between formal systems and ontological systems, including the *prima facie* differences I have noted above, the distinction between system and model is worth discussing in some detail. I shall begin by remarking that to the logician primarily concerned with the construction of formal systems, this distinction may seem clear; clear enough, in any event, not to give rise to practical difficulties. From the point of view of such a logician, a model is not itself a system; it is rather a situation that must be grasped intuitively. On the other hand, he may suppose that any system as such is capable of being developed without appeal to intuition.

At a somewhat more theoretical level, however, it is difficult to maintain this point of view. For the use of any situation as a model presupposes that it has already been interpreted, and this interpretation must always be more or less abstract. Let us suppose, for example, that the fragmentary system that I discussed earlier has been developed in such a way as to make clear the fact that the structure of the system does not depend upon any specific content to which the system might be applied. This could be done by using "$\phi(a, b)$" to express the idea that a is

related to b by any appropriate relation ϕ. "$\phi(a, b)$" may mean
"a is to the right of b"; it may also mean "a is to the left of b,"
"a is greater than b," "a is stronger than b," and so on. Then the
fragment that I wrote down before could be rewritten as follows.

   (1') If $\phi(a, b)$, then not $\phi(b, a)$

   (2') It is never the case that $\phi(a, a)$

   (3') If $\phi(a, b)$ and $\phi(b, c)$, then $\phi(a, c)$

Now suppose that someone were to cast about for a situation to
which (1') - (3') could be applied. He might decide upon the
following pattern of dots:

$$\cdot \quad \cdot \quad \cdot \quad \cdot \quad \cdot$$

He would then explain the applicability of, say, (2') to this pattern by pointing out that no dot is, in fact, to the right of itself.
But the difficulty is that *whether* any dot is, in fact, to the right
of itself depends upon what is meant by saying that one dot "is
to the right of" another. We might construe this relation in such
a way that a dot *could* be to the right of itself. In this case, (2')
is no longer satisfied by the pattern of dots. It may be objected,
of course, that "is to the right of" cannot be construed in this
way. This may be so. But if it is so, its being so does not follow
from anything that could be learned by inspecting the pattern
as such. It would follow only from the fact that *we think of* "is
to the right of" as an irreflexive relation; i.e., as a relation satisfying (2'). So the pattern is, after all, really irrelevant.

   As another example of the difficulty of maintaining that the
model has a simple and decisive role to play in the evalution of
formal systems, I shall call attention to the following design.

$\overline{\overline{xy}}$	$\overline{xy}$	xy	$\overline{x}y$	$\overline{\overline{x}\,\overline{y}}$
1	2	3	4	5

This design could serve as a model either for Boolean algebra
or for a very elementary system of serial order. I have used two
sets of labels to indicate these two entirely different interpretations.

   Perhaps it will be objected that the two rows of labels do
not, in fact, correspond to comparable aspects of the design: that

in one case we are concerned with regions, as in Venn diagrams, and in the other with successive entities that need not be represented as extended. But this is exactly my point. The design is not in itself the model of any system. It becomes a model only after it has been interpreted — as a collection of intersecting regions, for instance, or as a series of points. To interpret it, furthermore, is already to invest it with the properties of a formal system — properties from which the entire system could in fact be deduced. In theory, there is nothing to prevent any design whatever from serving as the model of any formal system whatever. If certain designs seem to lend themselves to certain interpretations more readily than to others, this is a psychological point rather than a logical one.

It may appear, then, that formal logic has no need for models — that it is concerned only with systems. In fact, however, models are indispensable. Not every deductive schema, for example, is valid in any given formal system. *Reductio ad absurdum,* as I have already pointed out, is valid in the fragmentary system I discussed, but invalid in many others. Indeed, the only systems that are, strictly speaking, formal are those in which the deductive schemata are unambiguously specified. But any such schema must necessarily correspond to a model; to the model, namely, that consists of the intuitively grasped language or metalanguage that contains or authorizes the schema in question. Of course, there is always the possibility of formalizing this language or metalanguage. But this procedure does not eliminate the model; it only postpones it to the next level. Even if the series of levels is infinite, we shall still have to depend upon the model that supplies an intuitive understanding of the law according to which the successive members of an infinite hierarchy are to be generated. I conclude that a purely abstract and nonintuitive formal system is no more a possibility than is a purely nonabstract model.

Yet even if there is no absolute distinction between system and model in formal logic, we are not entitled to censure the latter on this account. Formal logic never presupposes anything but a relative distinction. The logician employs models in order to evaluate systems, and makes use of systematic considerations in order to characterize various intuitively grasped situations. He tries to prove whatever is true, and to show the truth of whatever has been proved. There are decisive points at which a relative distinction between system and model becomes the basis for metalogical theorems concerning the scope or limits of decidability, provability, and so on. To each problem of this sort there corresponds a way of making the distinction that is sufficient to solve the problem in question. If we question the distinction, we are simply not addressing ourselves to any such problem. What I am trying to say here parallels Aristotle's remark that if we question the axioms of geometry, we are not addressing ourselves to geometrical problems. [2]

It seems appropriate to characterize the distinction that the logician makes between model and system as a *contingent relationship*. What I mean by this is that once he is presented with a formal system, the logician may well have to search for a model appropriate to it, and once he is confronted with a hitherto unsystematized situation, he may have to search for a way of systematizing its properties. Nor will he find either without luck. Even if there are occasions on which the required model or system is obvious, there is no way in which he can *infer* one from the other. This situation is reflected in the lack of general effective procedures for discovering proofs of consistency, as well as in the lack of general procedures for formalizing the properties even of those situations that seem most simple to intuition.

The commonplace that facts are contingent may be regarded as expressing an extension of the contingency of the model relatively to the system, provided that scientific knowledge is thought of as an all-inclusive system. Indeed, all of the main points I have made so far with respect to the role of the distinction between model and system in formal logic would apply equally well to logic in its broadest and least formal sense, as the general critique of arguments and statements. When we characterize a set of statements as inconsistent, for example, we cannot simply be referring to the systematic structure of the set, because an apparent inconsistency can often be resolved by making appropriate distinctions. [3] What we do mean is that no such distinc-

----

[2] See *Physics,* 185a 1-3

[3] On this point Strawson is particularly clear. See *Logical Theory* (London, 1952) p. 7

tions are possible; i.e., that the set has no model. Similarly, a statement is factually erroneous when it fails to correspond to any feature of the world, while belonging to a system of statements whose model allegedly is the world. (Reference to the model here is essential because factually erroneous statements must be distinguished from fictional ones, which do not take the world for a model.) A "material fallacy," such as equivocation, occurs when some of the statements involved in an argument, while appearing to belong to the same system, actually belong to different systems, as is shown by a lack of isomorphism among their models. "Formal fallacies" involve an obvious reference to a model. "P $\supset$ Q; Q; therefore, P" is fallacious in a system in which " $\supset$ " corresponds to the connective "only if" in the language serving as its model, but is valid if " $\supset$ " corresponds to "if." All of these types of error, furthermore, illustrate not only the relationship between model and system, but also the contingency of this relationship. The critique of ordinary discourse includes no infallible way of detecting such errors, which in fact come to our attention only in the light of an intuition whose contingency is often obvious. The fallacy seen by a politician in the oratory of his opponent may be a fallacy only with respect to a "model" of social reality or value intuited by the former but not by the latter. Models in disciplines whose objectivity is much less doubtful serve similarly in the criticism of argumentation within these disciplines. While it is true that in physics or chemistry the envisagement of a given model is scarcely a matter of individual temperament (as it perhaps is in the case of politics), but may rather characterize or even define the entire scientific community, this envisagement or intuition is still the result of discovery, not of deduction.

It would appear, then, that the presupposition of a distinction between system and model is involved in both formal and informal logic. On the other hand, I have tried to show that the distinction is open to question. As I have said, the question does not fall within the proper domain of logic. But it may still have its place. In the attempt to make clear what place it might have, I want to take it up again. Logic, I have said, presupposes a *contingent relationship* between system and model. The question that I was raising earlier, however, was whether the relationship between system and model need not be construed as *necessary*. I tried to show that in the absence of a system serving to control the interpretive process, it is impossible for any situation to constitute an unambiguous model; and that in the absence of a model, there can be no well-defined system, hence no system at all. Each determines the other in the sense that each is, strictly speaking, inconceivable in the absence of its counterpart. Thus, from the point of view of the question that I was raising and am here pursuing again, the problem of consistency vanishes. Any system, from this point of view, must have a model and so must be consistent. The same idea is expressed by saying that from this no doubt perverse-seeming point of view, all systems are absolutely consistent. This phraseology is intended as a reminder that from the point of view of logic, no system is ever more than relatively consistent: consistent, that is, relatively to a model that may or may not exist, and whose properties must themselves be assumed to be consistent. The logician who, in the hope of improving this state of affairs, attempts to formulate an absolutely consistent system will find that he is no longer engaged in a logical inquiry at all, but rather in an inquiry of the sort that I am trying to pursue.

But even if the distinction between system and model is open to question, what is the point of the question? Unless it has a point, it is wholly academic and of no greater importance than any of a host of other academic questions that might be raised. Yet there are moments when the question does have a point; namely, when it refers to ontological systems.

I have already tried to suggest that statements like "To be is to be perceived," "To be is to be an individual," and "To be is to be a material object" have systematic contexts. But what are the models of such systems? In particular, let us ask the man who asserts "To be is to be an individual" to answer this question for us. This man cannot be content merely to point to some one situation — say a certain collection of objects — for even if all the members of this collection were individuals, there would remain the possibility of other collections whose members were not individuals, and this possibility would be incompatible with the statement, "To be is to be an individual." Instead, he will have to say that the *world* — that is, everything that exists — is the model, and that whatever is not an individual does not belong to the world; it simply does not exist at all. Thus the system endorsed by this man determines its own model. At the same time, the model determines the system; for what the statement, "To be is to be an individual," fundamentally expresses is an intuition of the world as a collection of individuals. Thus it is that in ontology there is a necessary relationship between system and model.

Yet is it ever really necessary to utter ontological statements? If it is always possible, at least in principle, to avoid them, we have not yet advanced beyond a purely academic discussion. In my view, however, there are many occasions on which ontological statements are unavoidable. Some of these arise directly as the result of a concern with formal logic itself. It is possible, for example, for the logician to view with uneasiness that contingency of relationship between system and model of which I have been speaking. There is, after all, something unsatisfactory in the idea that the consistency of any given system amounts to more than the possibility of discovering a model for it. Discovery being a matter of contingency, who is to say what might or might not be discovered? In particular, what is there, in principle, to prevent the discovery of a model for any system whatever, thus establishing its consistency? But no logician supposes that the consistency of every system is capable of being established. In his view, there are many that fail to correspond to any situation to be found in the world; those, to wit, that are inconsistent.[4] But

---

[4] My point is similar to that of Kemeny's remark that "The question [of models] cannot be answered by first building a system and then defining what we mean by a model for that system. . . . We need a definition of what constitutes a model of any given system." ("Models of Logical Systems," *Journal of Symbolic Logic*, Vol. 13, 1948, p. 19) Kemeny goes on to provide a definition (*ibid.*, pp. 20-21) that is, as he says, "purely syntactic and applicable to all Logical Systems." (p. 21) But a purely syntactic definition stipulating "what constitutes a model of *any* given system" must be distinguished from the assertion that a model for a given system answering to this definition exists, thus establishing the consistency of the system. In saying this I am, in fact, simply repeating Kemeny's own definition of consistency: "A logical system is 'consistent' if it has a model." (p. 25)

It might nevertheless be tempting to suppose that one could determine whether models for various systems exist by referring only to a syntactic definition of "model." In particular, one might deliberately construct a system which, according to this definition, has no model. Would this sufat this juncture a new notion of consistency has entered the scene. The logician is now thinking of consistency in general as a correspondence between a given system and what there is in the real world, rather than as a correspondence between the system and any of an unrestricted range of possible models. But what is there in this world? Individuals? Classes? Minds? Material particles? Possibilities? The only possible reply is that the real world includes whatever exists, and nothing else. What, then, exists? An ontological question is no longer avoidable. It is a question, furthermore, to which we are led by a concern proper to formal logic itself. Similar concerns connected with such logical notions as truth,[5] provability, independence, completeness, and so on, as well as with the notion of consistency, will inevitably lead us to the same question or a similar one.

I do not know whether the account I have just given is sufficient to establish the necessity for ontological statements and systems, although I hope that it is. Yet whether it is theoretically sufficient or not, this account as it now stands is unlikely to put to rest certain perplexities that may be raised by my characterization of such statements and systems. I have said, for example, that ontological systems determine their own models. But is it really possible for any system to do this? It is tempting to suppose that given a system, the question of whether there exists anything capable of serving as its model is a question of fact. Yet what this criticism overlooks is that every ontology claims to define the conditions under which anything is to be regarded as a fact. For the ontology according to which to be is to be an individual, for example, to report a fact is to make a true state-

---

4 (Continued)
fice to show that not every system is consistent? If so, then it is possible to avoid appealing to the real world in the attempt to establish that point. But the question of interpreting the symbols of the constructed system remains, and it is clear that there will be some interpretations (i.e., models in my sense) on which any such system could be regarded as consistent, provided that such interpretations have a place in the real world. This is true even for the point of view from which the question of interpretation does not arise — a point of view that identifies logic with syntax — for this point of view presupposes that some symbols and sequences of symbols, but not all, have a place in the real world.

5 For a thoughtful development of the ontological implications of a formal treatment of truth, see F. Crahay, "Sémantique et Métaphysique," *Logique et Analyse*, old series, No. 7, 1956, pp. 19-27

ment regarding an individual or several of them, and nothing else. To criticize this ontology for disregarding what it cannot on its own principles regard as a matter of fact is to beg the question.

It is an essential characteristic of all models, whether in logic or in ontology, that they are grasped intuitively. It is peculiar to ontology, however, that the intuition of the model is directly regulated by the system itself, instead of remaining adventitious, as it is in logic. Perhaps this is why ontology is sometimes thought to depend upon innate, or self-confirming, ideas rather than upon adventitious ideas. In any event, when an ontological system is criticized on the basis of alleged facts, the real issue is likely to be the difference between the intuitions of the critic and those involved in the ontology which he is attacking. But while the critic's intuitions answer only to a system casually seized upon and half-consciously apprehended, those of his adversary answer to the principles of an explicit ontology. The advantage seems to rest, therefore, with the latter.

It is, however, an advantage that cuts both ways. For the advocate of an ontological system is no more entitled to appeal to facts than is his critic. The only facts available to the man who asserts "To be is to be an individual," for instance, are reports about individuals. But the attempt to establish or defend the assertion in question by appealing to such reports is just as question-begging as is the attempt to refute it by appealing to reports of another sort.

It is clear, furthermore, that logical considerations have no more weight in the criticism or defense of an ontological system than do factual considerations. The consistency of such a system is guaranteed by the model that it itself supplies. Any attempt, therefore, to *prove* that the system is consistent is certain to beg the question at one point or another; and any attempt to prove that it is inconsistent can amount to no more than a simple denial that any appropriate model exists — a denial that once again begs the question.

It might appear, then — and this is a second perplexity — that it is impossible to argue either for or against an ontological system. If only one such system had ever been proposed, this might not seem to be a difficulty, because we should probably regard its constituent statements as trivially true in the sense in which we regard tautologies as trivially true. Indeed, the claim has been made that the tautology reveals the structure of the world.[6] Yet, whether or not this solution could be viewed as satisfactory, it is unavailable. For more than one ontological system has in fact been proposed, and commitment to any one of them entails rejection of all or most of the others. A little later I want to indicate why it is not obvious that this conflict should occur, and to suggest one rather unobvious reason for its occurrence. For the moment, it is interesting to note that formal systems do not conflict with one another at all, at least in the way ontological systems do. No one claims, for example, that Boolean algebra is incompatible with projective geometry, and no one attempts to eliminate the latter in favor of the former or vice versa. Of course, it may be claimed that one systematic formulation of Boolean algebra, departing from one set of postulates, is superior to another that departs from another set, but, if so, the claim is only that the former is superior in some limited respect or group of respects, not that the latter is altogether untenable and must accordingly be eliminated.

Must one finally settle for a plurality of conflicting ontologies whose conflicts can never be resolved? This situation would be unavoidable if the appeal to evidence and the appeal to logic were the only resources available for resolving ontological conflicts; for whenever such an appeal is made, at least one party to the dispute can reject it as question-begging. But there may be another resource; namely, the possibility of overthrowing a system that one attacks not by attempting to confront it with statements whose truth it cannot acknowledge, but rather by confronting it with statements whose truth it must acknowledge. This possibility is easy to document. I spoke earlier of a logician whose uneasiness about the general notion of consistency has led him to think of consistency as a correspondence between a given system and what there is in the real world, rather than as a correspondence between the system and any of an unrestricted range of possible models. This logician is accordingly forced to espouse an ontological system, although the data I have so far given are,

---

[6] See Wittgenstein, *Tractatus Logico-Philosophicus* (London, 1922), especially 6.124 and 6.13

of course, by no means sufficient to indicate which one of a variety of relevant systems he must espouse. Let us assume that he has in fact elected to characterize what there is in the real world by saying, "To be is to be an individual." (This is, in any event, an ontological statement commonly enough made by contemporary logicians.) The point, then, is that his commitment to a specific ontological system is dictated by an intention to explicate the general notion of consistency. Yet it may be possible for those who advocate ontological systems in conflict with this one to argue that precisely because the logician in question has asserted "To be is to be an individual," his intention cannot be satisfied. Perhaps there are areas of formal logic whose existence he cannot deny and in which it would be impossible to explicate the notion of consistency if the real world contained individuals only.

Now this argument makes no appeal either to evidence — at least, to evidence of any type that I have considered so far — or to formal logic. There is a sense, of course, in which the assertion of the existence of certain areas of formal logic is a report of evidence. But unlike other such reports whose role (or lack of a role) in ontological conflict I have been considering, this one cannot be rejected as question-begging. It is a statement whose truth the logician to whom it is addressed must acknowledge, because his intention was to explicate the notion of consistency in general; i.e., as applying to all areas of formal logic. He may, of course, reply that those areas in which the notion of consistency cannot be explicated if the real world contains individuals only do not themselves exist. If this reply amounts to nothing more than a restatement of the assertion "To be is to be an individual," then his antagonists may properly accuse him of begging the question. If, on the other hand, it is based upon an independent ontological thesis — in this case, perhaps, the thesis that no more than a denumerable infinity of things exist — then the issue will have to be joined in different terms. The point, however, is that the issue *can* be joined.

That the same argument makes no appeal to formal logic is shown by the fact that the dispute itself centers upon the notion of formal consistency. The argument is successful if it exhibits an incompatibility between the intention to explicate the general notion of consistency and the assertion "To be is to be an individual." One cannot, therefore, regard this incompatibility as itself a case of formal inconsistency without begging the question, i.e., assuming that the nature of formal consistency has already been decided upon. In more general and more generally applicable terms, of course, the incompatibility I am here alluding to cannot be formal inconsistency simply because the systematic context of "To be is to be an individual" is absolutely consistent from the point of view of formal logic. Nothing that exists, in other words, is formally inconsistent with it.

The argument, then, appeals to the intentions of the logician to whom it is addressed, rather than to evidence or formal logic. One may say that the logic of the argument is a logic of intentions or motives. My view is that it is only through the use of this logic that ontological conflicts can be resolved. Indeed, in the absence of such a logic it is difficult to understand how conflict over ontological systems could even be described. In writing this chapter, I have, of course, been assuming that they could. But there is still the question of whether what I have written makes sense. What I have written does not make sense — or at least is very difficult to understand — if it is possible to say no more about the relationships among ontological systems than that each claims to be absolutely consistent and that each claims to include all the evidence. For in this situation no system can even acknowledge the existence of a threat to its own status. Thus it is hard to see how ontological systems could be in conflict with each other at all. One cannot say, as one is perhaps tempted to, that two or more ontological systems are in conflict from some point of view that includes both or all. For each system in turn can be regarded as precisely the denial that such a point of view exists, and to disregard this denial is to beg the question. Nor can one properly ascribe the conflict to the fact that the parties to it make incompatible statements about one and the same situation — to wit, the world; for, as I have already indicated, nothing in principle prevents the same situation from serving as the model for different systems. Ontological conflict does make sense only in terms of the very considerations that must be used to resolve it; that is, in terms of a logic of intentions. Ontological systems can deny each other, but only if each denial is an at least implicit argument directing attention to an incoherence between the content of the system denied and the intentions of its advocates. This is actually just a special case of the conclusion to which I was led in Chapter II. There I tried to show that not only ontological conflict, but philosophical disagreement in general, presupposes the exchange of arguments of this sort — an exchange for which I adopted the term "controversy." In Chapters III through VII, I have attempted to describe and evaluate the sorts of arguments involved in philosophical controversy.

Now I want to consider whether the developments of this chapter shed any light upon the previously mentioned *prima facie* differences between ontological and formal systems. First, the grounds of ontological statements cannot consist of "postulates" because in a system whose relation to its model is necessary there is no distinction between postulates and theorems. There is such a distinction only when it is possible to focus attention upon the system in its own right, without reference to any model; i.e., when the relation between the model and the system is contingent. But it is self-deception to pretend to have proved theorems on the basis of postulates when both postulates and theorems are in fact directly read from a model that one cannot avoid envisaging whenever one envisages the system. Writers who have attempted to pursue the Geometrical Method in philosophy are often criticized for just this sort of self-deception.[7] It is clear, in any event, that precisely the criticisms that can be brought to bear against ontological "theorems" can also be brought to bear against the "postulates" that are alleged to support them, so that when the grounds of an ontological statement are demanded, the demand is never satisfied by exhibiting ontological "postulates." When such "postulates" are adduced, it is natural that they should themselves become the locus of the issue.

The second difference was that ontological systems do not seem to be especially vulnerable to logical criticism. This situation owes itself to the absolute consistency of such systems. No

---

[7] See, for example, G. H. R. Parkinson, *Spinoza's Theory of Knowledge* (Oxford, 1954) p. 21

doubt ontological systems are often infelicitously expressed; perhaps they always are. Accordingly the language in which they are expressed may have to be revised. But the criticism that occasions such revisions, to the extent that it arises from the traditional critique of statements and arguments — from the organon of logic, formal and informal — cannot touch the system itself more than superficially, for the relation between system and model presupposed by this organon does not obtain here.

Finally, there is the fact that while the distinction between proof and truth is important in formal logic, it seems to have no place in ontology. This is explained by pointing out that the distinction between proof and truth arises from the contingent relationship between system and model. The process of proof makes no reference to the existence or properties of any model. Analogously the assertion of truth is not intended to refer beyond the intuitively grasped situation to which it applies. But if the system entails its own model, the distinction in question can no longer be maintained.

IX

Argumentation and Selfhood

I have been arguing, as well as making use of the conclusion, that all valid philosophical arguments are addressed *ad hominem*. This conclusion will be an assumption of the discussion I now want to undertake. Another assumption that I shall make is that it is obligatory for at least one person to accept the conclusion of a valid philosophical argument. I have discussed this point in Chapter IV. In addition, I want to assume that these two assumptions are related; that is, that the persons obligated to accept the conclusion of a valid philosophical argument are precisely those to whom it is addressed, *ad hominem*. This assumption does not seem implausible; it is difficult, in fact, to imagine how those obligated to accept the conclusion of an *argumentum ad hominem* could be *other* than the *homines* to whom the argument is addressed.

What I should like to do now is to consider whether the obligation of a person to accept the conclusion of a valid *argumentum ad hominem* reveals anything about the person so obligated. Obligations of other types obviously reveal something about those obligated. An almost trivial illustration is provided by the fact that it is only to human beings that obligations can be ascribed at all. This shows an important difference between human beings and animals. At a more specific level, some people have obligations that others do not, and these obligations reveal something about these people in particular. The politician, the parent, and the bus driver, for example, have special obligations. Not everyone is obligated to an electorate, a set of children, or a group of passengers. Of course, everyone does have these obligations to the extent that he is a politician, parent, or bus driver. To pursue one of these careers is to be chargeable with the obligations that are special to it. To be a parent is, at least in part, to be obligated to one's children. But this means that an account of parental obligations would disclose something about what it is like to be a parent. Indeed, the only adequate reply that many parents can think of when asked "What is it like to be a parent?" consists of an enumeration of the special obligations incumbent upon parents. It goes without saying that no such enumeration could reveal *all* that there is to the state of parenthood. Another account, for example, would describe the singular felicity or infelicity of this state. But the story of what the parent, and no one else, is obligated to do, would still constitute an indispensable part of any general characterization of parenthood.

One way in which the enumeration of a parent's obligations sheds light on the nature of parenthood is that it calls attention to a parent's *commitment*. Under conventional circumstances, at least, to become a parent is willy-nilly to be committed to supporting and rearing one's children. The special obligations of the parent arise from this commitment, and the reason they are special to parents is that most nonparents have not made the commitment. Of course, some nonparents do make the commitment in question, as when they adopt children. But the moment they do, they automatically assume the role of parent, with all of its obligations. This suggests that obligations are obligations only relatively to commitments.

I want to turn now to my main task of discussing the *homo* who is obligated to accept the conclusion of the *argumentum ad hominem* addressed to him. As in the case of the parent, no account of this individual's special obligations vis-à-vis philosophical argumentation could be a sufficient basis for a *complete* characterization of what it is to engage in philosophical argumentation. Just as an alternative story about parenthood could be launched from an account of parental felicity or infelicity, so an alternative story — involving such themes as philosophical inspiration, wonder, and doubt — might be told about the philosophical arguer. Yet the characterization based upon the obligations of the arguer is an essential part of the complete characterization. As in the case of the parent, this characterization will be largely an elucidation of the commitment to which the obligations in question are relative.

In order to ascertain the commitments of the philosophical arguer, I want to begin by asking why a person to whom a valid *argumentum ad hominem* is addressed is obligated to accept the conclusion of the argument. It is tempting to reply, "Just because the argument is valid." This reply is certainly not incorrect, but at the same time it is not very revealing. At least one person, and in most cases every person, is, after all, obligated to accept the conclusion of *any* valid argument, whether it be addressed *ad hominem* or not. So the reply does not suggest any circumstances peculiar to the *argumentum ad hominem* that in particular obligate the person to whom it is addressed to accept its conclusion when it is valid. A more satisfactory reply must take as its point of departure those characteristics of a valid *argumentum ad hominem* by virtue of which it is valid, and must then proceed to show how it is precisely these characteristics — not the characteristics of valid arguments in general — that give rise to the obligation to accept the conclusion of the argument.

It is perhaps by reviewing my previous remarks about why an *argumentum ad hominem* has force that I can best explain why there is, in particular, an obligation to accept its conclusion. The force of an *argumentum ad hominem* arises from the seriousness with which the person to whom it is addressed is attempting to make a point, argue a case, or defend a position. Aristotle was able to show the self-defeating nature of Eudoxus' argument by insisting that since Eudoxus intended this argument seriously, he had to take a closely similar argument seriously. Aristotle was not attempting to prove anything; he was merely showing what Eudoxus was bound to admit in conformity with his own principles of reasoning. Similarly, Hume is appealing to the principles of reasoning employed by the Cartesians when he shows that the same principle that led them to deny that matter possesses power should also have led them to deny that God can possess it. Like Aristotle, Hume too is doing something quite different from attempting to establish a positive conclusion. What he is doing

would have no point unless the argument of the Cartesians had
been seriously put forward.

Eudoxus, then, is obligated to endorse an argument closely
similar to his own, and hence to conclude that the latter is self-
defeating, because this closely similar argument achieves its close
similarity by conforming exactly to Eudoxus' own principles of
reasoning. In other words, Eudoxus' obligation arises simply
from his commitment to a principle of reasoning. Analogously,
the Cartesians are obligated to accept the conclusion of Hume's
argument just because they are committed to a principle of reasoning to which the latter conforms. The obligation in each case
is clearly relative to the commitment. Only those reasoning as
Eudoxus does would be obligated to accept the conclusion of
Aristotle's argument, and similarly for Hume's. I shall maintain
that the obligation to accept the conclusion of a valid philosophical *argumentum ad hominem* is always relative to a similar commitment. If what the critic is attacking is an argument, the
commitment exploited will be a commitment to the principles of
reasoning essential to the argument under attack. But, as I have
tried to show, valid philosophical *argumenta ad hominem* can
attack statements as well as arguments. When they do, the commitments in question will be commitments to the points of view
expressed by the statements. Thus the attack upon the statement
"All knowledge is the function of the adjustment of the organism
to its environment" presupposes that those who make this statement are committed to the general position it expresses.

What I have said so far can be summarized by the statement
that the obligation to accept valid criticism of one's philosophical
point of view stems directly from one's commitment to the point
of view itself. One can think of this obligation as special: it is
incumbent only upon those who have philosophical commitments,
just as parental obligations affect only those who have parental
commitments. But in the case of the philosophical obligations,
this way of thinking of the matter puts a strain on the word
"special." There are certainly nonparents. But are there really
any human beings who lack philosophical commitments? To
transform this rhetorical question into a confident declarative
sentence would require voluminous discussion falling mostly beyond the scope of this book. Yet it is possible to mention some

considerations upon which such a transformation might rest. One is a point to which I made passing reference a little earlier; namely, that man is the only animal to whom obligations can be ascribed. A stronger statement is at least nearly as plausible: to be human is to have obligations. For practices of many sorts presuppose not only that obligation falls to the lot of man alone, but also that it falls to the lot of every man. Not only do we not ascribe obligations to animals, but in addition whenever we are confronted with a being to whom it is impossible to ascribe obligations, we are reluctant to accord it full human status. Now since obligation is relative to commitment, this stronger statement implies that to be human is to have commitments. Among the commitments consciously or unconsciously made by any human being, there will be some of considerable generality. A person hardly can commit himself to detailed arrangements and projects unless he is to some extent already committed to a general way of life from which the arrangements and projects acquire their significance. But surely it requires no stretching of the adjective "philosophical" to apply it to a commitment to a general way of life.

It may be objected that what I have just said still does not show that all men share the obligations that fall to those who engage in philosophical argumentation. For while commitment to a way of life can be unsophisticated, undeliberate, and even altogether unconscious, the obligation to accept the conclusion of a valid philosophical *argumentum ad hominem* must require a sophisticated, deliberate, and fully conscious commitment. The reply, however, is that this is simply not so. Nothing in the concept of a valid *argumentum ad hominem* requires the person addressed by the argument to be clear about or in control of the commitment that the argument exploits. Indeed, the very effect of the argument may well be to render clear the hitherto unclear commitment of the person addressed, and thereby to place in his hands the power to assert or revise it deliberately. Philosophers from Plato to Wittgenstein have held that the chief use of valid philosophical argumentation is as a reminder of commitments that one party to the argument has already made. Furthermore, there is no general commitment to a way of life that could not be involved in a valid *argumentum ad hominem* in precisely

the way in which sophisticated, deliberate, conscious commitments are involved. Whenever a man's conduct, or some specific
course of action that he has recommended, can be shown to be
incompatible with the general way of life to which he is committed (whether or not he knows that he is committed to it), the
pattern of the argument showing the incompatibility is essentially the same as the pattern of the more technically philosophical
argumenta ad hominem considered in detail in previous chapters.

It is considerations of this sort, I think, that tend to show
that the obligations of those who engage in philosophical argumentation are, unlike those of the parent, of general rather than
special applicability. Since they are general, and since obligations reveal something about the nature of those obligated, the
obligations of the arguer must disclose something about human
nature as such, rather than just about some special class of people, such as parents or bus drivers. This chapter could have been
entitled "Argumentation and Human Nature," and in fact will
not depart from the subject denoted by that title. My only reason
for preferring "Selfhood" to "Human Nature" is that the particular
aspects of human nature primarily revealed by the study of the
obligations of those who engage in philosophical arguments are,
for the most part, traditionally regarded as aspects of selfhood.
To such aspects I now turn.

The first is *reflection.* It is often asserted that the capacity
to reflect upon its own commitments is essential to the self. This
capacity is clearly related to the obligations of a person to whom
a valid *argumentum ad hominem* is addressed, because one thing
the argument obligates him to do is to become aware of the ramifications of his own philosophical commitment. If the capacity
of the self to reflect had hitherto passed unnoted, discussion of
this obligation would certainly disclose it, because the obligation
would make no sense without the capacity. Reflection is thus one
of the aspects of selfhood that is revealed by the obligations of
the arguer.

The notion of the *reflexivity* of the self is closely related to
that of its obligation to reflect. A thoughtful person is likely to
be committed to a point of view that includes beliefs about his
own nature or role. Philosophical criticism can remind him of his
own commitment to such beliefs. When it does, self-examination

is obligatory. One powerful type of argument consists in showing that a person's view of his own selfhood is incompatible with the possibility of his asserting that view. For example, the assertion that the self is merely a bundle of sense-impressions and moral sentiments seems to presuppose that the self is in fact something else; namely, an *observer* of its own content of sense-impressions and moral sentiments. Philosophers from Kant to Ryle have noticed how the interplay between the self as observed content and the self as the observer of this content gives rise to an infinite regress. The observation that there is an observer seems to presuppose a further observer to make the observation. One rather drastic way of overcoming this regress is to posit a fundamental distinction between an empirical self, which can be observed but which can never achieve reflexivity, and a transcendental ego, fully reflexive but never the object of any observation. In my own view, a fully reflexive self is no more a possibility than is a self completely aware of the ramifications of its commitments. Both strike me as unattainable ideals, no less ideals for being unattainable.

A valid *argumentum ad hominem* does more than merely remind a person of his own commitments and their ramifications. It also obligates him to abandon or revise those commitments. Having seen the limitations of his principles of reasoning or point of view, he must move on to something more adequate. This is, I think, part of what is meant by saying that man is the only animal that can transcend itself. Of course the phrase "self-transcendence" may refer simply to man's ability to talk about his own environment or way of life; in order to talk about it, he must already occupy a position beyond it. This sense of "self-transcendence" is already covered by what I have said about reflection. It is the literature of existentialism that suggests that man's self-transcendence is more than a capacity to reflect upon the world and his situation in it. From a Heideggerian point of view, the act of transcending the world is also the act of losing it. One cannot take a position vis-à-vis the world without at the same time seeing that position as essentially precarious. It is threatened by its own ramifications. The position slips away, and nothing remains. The nothing that remains is perhaps partly a radical incompatibility. If this is so (and I am by no means confident of

my exegesis), then the human condition of "anguish" is at least
to some extent a sense that any commitment that one could make
is incompatible with its own ramifications.

Self-transcendence might lead to anguish in a person who
suddenly came to be quite certain that every philosophical commitment is doomed. But it is not necessary to think of self-
transcendence as always having this shattering effect. One may
instead think of it as giving rise to a gradual transition from
naïveté to sophistication. I shall refer to such a transition as
"personal history." Such history is the story of how an individual,
by complying with his obligation to discard inadequate principles
and positions once their inadequacies were made clear to him,
made more nearly adequate commitments, and so participated in
the process of growing up. He saw his commitments as doomed
one by one, while the anguished person sees his own as doomed
all at once. It is clearly legitimate to think of personal history as
an aspect of selfhood, at least if one does not endorse a theory
of the self to which anguish is fundamental. Even if one does
endorse such a theory, one may still regard personal history as
a way of looking at the self, albeit a perverse and bourgeois way
that sees the successful thinker as a philosophical Horatio Alger.

So far, I have said nothing about the interpersonal aspects
of selfhood. It is often asserted that the self depends for its
realization or even its existence upon active membership in a
human community. If there is an obligation to criticize, as well
as to respond to criticism, then the view of argumentation that I
have been defending would have some connection with this side
of the story. I have already asserted that to be human is to have
commitments. Since the commitments of different people can be
mutually incompatible, this leads to the problem of philosophical
disagreement. That problem, as I tried to show in Chapter II,
can be resolved only through genuine controversy. Thus anyone
who believes that the difference between his own commitments
and those of others creates a problem is obligated, by virtue of
his commitment to this belief in particular, to engage in controversy. One cannot at one and the same time believe that one has
a problem and believe that one has no obligation to attempt to
solve it. So whoever is committed to a view not shared by everyone is obligated to criticize those commitments with which he

disagrees. In so doing, he contributes to the self-transcendence of others and invites others to contribute to his own self-transcendence. Nor is this interaction in any way incidental to the process of self-transcendence. In order to transcend himself, a person must be confronted with an *argumentum ad hominem.* He will be so confronted only if someone else is interested in arguing against him. This presupposes at least one other individual who feels that a difference between philosophical positions is worth arguing about.

A further and equally important interpersonal aspect of selfhood is the aspect that is indicated by the assertion that to be a self one must *respect* other selves. This aspect is connected with the obligation to accept the protest that one has begged the question in arguing against the position of another, supposing that the protest is valid. If one is obligated to accept such a protest, then one is obligated not to beg the question in the first place. But to beg the question in philosophical disputation is to miss the point of one's antagonists' assertions. It is to deal cavalierly, thus disrespectfully, with his commitment. Respect, on the other hand, is conveyed by the use of arguments that do not miss the point. A community can be fully human only when each member criticizes the others in terms of the ramifications of commitments that are actually theirs. It seems to me that this sort of community is essentially democratic.

One commonly discussed aspect of selfhood that may appear to be independent of the aspects I have touched upon so far is power. It is at least as plausible to regard the self as the locus of a quest for power as to think of it as striving for stable commitments or respect. There is a point of view, furthermore, from which the two quests appear to be radically distinct. Power may be seen as a manifestation of will, and commitment and respect as a manifestation of reason — pure or practical, as the case may be. I have no intention of offering one more putative solution of the problem of the relation between will and reason. But I think I can show that the view of argumentation I have been advocating has as much connection with power as with the intellectual aspects of selfhood.

One way of suggesting the connection I have in mind is by explaining why I think that any theory of philosophical controversy that takes an exclusively intellectualistic view of the self, thus failing to connect controversy with something like the quest for power, is bound to break down. First, a terminological point. The advocate of a purely intellectualistic view would probably hesitate to think of philosophical argumentation as basically a matter of "commitments." The word "commitment" already has nonintellectual overtones. It suggests the endorsement of a principle or position through an act of will rather than through an act of knowledge. Of course, the intellectualist need not suppose that positions are taken as the result of any ordinary kind of knowledge. He may prefer to use the word "insight" to refer to philosophical knowledge. I shall for the moment follow his lead, but I shall leave open the question whether philosophical insight is ordinary or extraordinary knowledge. On either alternative, intellectualistic views of philosophical controversy can be divided into two main classes. They tend either to doubt that argumentation results in a net gain in insight or to hope that it may. The doubtful theories are exemplified by Hume, Kant, and Logical Positivism.[1] Such positions are characterized by a polemical zeal that is incomprehensible and morally impossible unless it is genuinely motivated by the desire to promote new insights. The philosophical argument to the effect that philosophical arguments make no contribution is surely itself intended as a contribution, and so undercuts itself.

The hopeful theories of philosophical controversy would be represented by traditional views of dialectic prior to Kant. The common theme here appears to be the assumption that philosophical disagreements can be resolved within a universe of discourse that includes each of the opposing philosophies, and whose discovery enlarges human insight.[2] What such theories overlook is that philosophical antagonism may be so radical as to preclude any but the most trivial reconciliation of this kind. To what

---

[1] In more recent times, a view of this sort has been expressed by Richard McKeon. See, for example, "Philosophy and Method," *The Journal of Philosophy*, Vol. 48, 1951, pp. 653-682.

[2] One of the staunchest latter-day expositors of this theme is Mortimer Adler. From his early book *Dialectic* (New York, Harcourt Brace & Co., 1927) through *The Idea of Freedom* (Garden City, N. Y., Doubleday & Co., 1958), Adler has been proposing universes of discourse within which philosophical controversies can be resolved.

fruitful universe of discourse, for example, can the conflicting assertions of the theist and the atheist be referred? The real rub, of course, is that the hopeful theories are themselves irrevocably opposed by the doubtful ones. Resolution of this issue would require the discovery of a universe of discourse in which, *per impossibile,* doubt and hope reduce to the same thing.[3]

If there is a deadlock between two theories, one of which asserts that philosophical controversies can enhance philosophical insight and the other that they cannot, the deadlock can be overcome by denying that philosophical controversies are geared to the enhancement of philosophical insight in the first place. But this denial need not be interpreted as the denial that there is any connection at all between the arguments of philosophers and the enhancement of insight. Such enhancement might be the *result* of controversy, even if not the *purpose* of it.

Without further ado, I shall introduce my own view that philosophical controversy is one of the channels through which a person may seek power. One important feature of the kind of power that the arguer attempts to secure is that it is bilateral. It is power that one can possess only by granting it to others. For there is no dispute at all unless each participant is willing to be corrected by precisely the same principles that he uses to correct the others. If *I* condemn *your* philosophy for violating the Law of Contradiction or the Principle of Parsimony, then *I* am obligated to accept *your* charge that *my* view itself fails to satisfy these standards. For *your* charge, if it does not miss the point, will then be a valid *argumentum ad hominem.* Furthermore, even if all that I have said on behalf of the use of argumentation of this type were to be rejected, this requirement of reciprocity could still be justified. For criticism that applied only in one direction would be a mark of insincerity. What is more important, such unilateral criticism would betray its own impotence. For if the critic himself is immune to it, then clearly it cannot have the general effectiveness that any critical principle, to be valid, must have.

Bilateral power contrasts with most of the usual kinds of power, such as physical force, control through reward and pun-

---

[3] I have, of course, already criticized the "hopeful" theories — from a slightly different point of view — in Chapter II. See pp. 15-16

ishment, persuasion through propaganda, and brainwashing.
These are essentially unilateral in that the exercise of such power
is impaired if the exerciser himself is subjected to the power he
exercises. In philosophical controversy, on the other hand, the
power of a given disputant is enhanced by his subjection to it,
because that subjection serves to increase the number of critical
principles available for his own use.

I do not mean to suggest, however, that philosophy is the
only area in which bilateral power occurs. There are, in fact, at
least two others, and the problem now is to distinguish the conflicts arising in these areas from those in which philosophers are
involved. The first such area is that of scientific and common-
sense knowledge. Power here is bilateral in the sense that whoever undertakes to correct or supplement what another asserts
in the name of knowledge must be willing to be instructed by
that other person. This is a part of the meaning of the statement
that scientists are impartial. Impartiality in this sense is essential
to the scientific outlook. If pride, or some deeper source of partiality, prevents me from accepting the facts you convey to me,
you will be properly suspicious that the "facts" that I tell you
are colored by the same partiality.

These very remarks about bilateral power in science and
common-sense knowledge, however, are intended to suggest a
difference between this area and that of philosophical controversy. For the latter does not depend upon facts, at least in the
way in which science and common-sense knowledge depend upon
them. In the course of an argument, the scientist, businessman,
nature lover, or baseball enthusiast might well learn something
that surprised him. The person who produced the fact might
even win the argument. But nothing surprises the philosopher
in this way. For his very point of view can be interpreted as a
definition of factuality; and whatever should fall external to that
would not be a fact at all. Another way to put this point is to
repeat that while the statements involved in the corpus of scientific and common-sense knowledge are true or false independently
of the arguments used to reach them, the truth or falsity of philosophical statements is relative to argument.

Formal logic is the second area that I had in mind in which
bilateral power occurs. The logician, like the scientist, must be

impartial. He will engage in a reciprocal critique involving such notions as implication, consistency, and independence. But just as the philosopher is undisturbed by criticism based upon facts, so will he be largely unmoved by the discovery of purely logical flaws in the statements he has made in the course of a dispute. It is characteristic of a genuine philosophical outlook in which logical flaws have been found to experience no difficulty in reformulating itself to avoid the flaws. The role of logic in the elaboration of a philosophical view is regulative, not constitutive. While logic is often a centrally important device for expressing philosophical positions in an orderly manner (I hope that my use of logic in this book, for example, will be judged in that light), it is usually not the use of logic that leads the philosopher to maintain his position in the first place. Philosophical positions are rarely, if ever, inferred, although for expository purposes they may be represented as the products of inference.

The point I am trying to make may be summarized by saying that the sort of power the philosopher seeks to secure is enhanced neither by the possession of facts nor by the capacity to engage in logical criticism. Perhaps the most important requirement for the enhancement of this sort of power is a grasp of the philosophical commitments of those whom one seeks to control. The most powerful philosophical critic is the one who is most adept at participating histrionically in the positions he criticizes. A philosophy can be refuted only by someone sympathetic to it. Another requirement is the inadvertent cooperation of the person whose philosophical position is under attack; for the position can be destroyed only through his very advocacy of it. Philosophical criticism can make no appeal whatsoever to the relaxed mind. It is "control over another only insofar as he is in control of himself."[4]

The possibility of a person's inadvertently bringing about the downfall of his position as the result of the seriousness of his advocacy of it is at least reminiscent of the Greek paradigm for the operation of fate. Since fate, in the Greek version at any rate, is closely associated with selfhood, a further link between philosophical argumentation and selfhood is suggested. In order

---

[4] This is the phrase of Professor J. W. Miller of Williams College.

to bring out this link, I should like to conclude by comparing
the philosopher with the hero of Sophocles' *Oedipus the King*.

As soon as he had learned of the fate that lay in store for
him, Oedipus embarked upon a desperate attempt to avoid it.
This attempt, however, was precisely what brought his fate down
upon him. Similarly, positions are taken in philosophy in order
to avoid a clearly perceived fate. For the philosopher, as for
Oedipus, this fate takes the form of involvement in an inhuman
situation; the philosopher seeks to avoid the arrogance, slovenliness, pettiness, cynicism, or doubt that threatens to dehumanize
his thought. But just as for Oedipus, the philosopher's attempt
to avoid his fate serves only to drive him deeper into its toils.
Having fled inhumanity, he finds that he has become all the more
monstrously inhuman. For among the ramifications of his commitment, there may well be far worse evils than the arrogance
or slovenliness that made him take refuge in this commitment.

Like Oedipus, the philosopher often stands upon the dreaded
brink of discovery. The moments of philosophical discovery are
the occasions upon which the philosopher engages in genuine
controversy. He cannot avoid controversy any more than Oedipus
could avoid interrogating those who held the fatal clues. At first,
he may shrug off criticism, as Oedipus shrugged off the statements of Teiresias. Many philosophers never pass beyond this
phase. The fate of inhumanity has already fallen upon them.
But others are filled with an increasing anxiety to know the worst.

We may want to say that Oedipus was the victim of his own
impetuousness, or that the fate that befell him was arbitrary and
cruel. Neither of these statements, however, permits us to understand Oedipus as a man. It would be cowardly to refuse to act
without complete knowledge of the consequences of action, or
to blame the consequences, once they descended, on anyone else.
One respects Oedipus both for his attempt to escape and for
taking full responsibility for the disaster that this attempt brings
about. Similarly, the philosopher who dreads inhumanity must
not be cowardly, for this is a mode of precisely the inhumanity
he dreads. Even if his work is destined to bear inhuman fruit,
he must perform it like a man. It would appear that in order
to be human, one must always be passing from one inhuman act
to another.

It was necessary for Oedipus to learn what fate was in store for him; for if he had not learned, the fate would not have been fulfilled. Even if the fated events had occurred, they would have occurred as misfortune, not as fate. Thus the complete statement of Oedipus' fate must refer to itself. It must assert, in effect, "The fate of Oedipus is to slay his father and wed his mother, *and to know that this is his fate.*" The argument fatal to a philosophical position also has a self-referential character. The philosopher's fate cannot fall upon him unless he not only resists inhumanity, but also is aware that resistance to inhumanity is his task. For if he does not see the resistance as a task, he cannot see the culminating inhumanity as a failure. In this case, he will be immune to any fatal argument. And such immunity is the ultimate inhumanity that strips him of his very status as philosopher, just as Oedipus could not have been a man if he had not struggled against his fate.

The paradigm of arguments fatal to philosophical positions, then, is the charge that the philosopher has adopted a mode of inhumanity in his very attempt to avoid inhumanity. The arguments which I have characterized as valid throughout this book are those that fall under this paradigm. One relation between argumentation of this sort and selfhood, then, is that the person who responds to such argumentation reveals his own humanity — and inhumanity — in his response. Character is response to fate.

Index

A

Adler, M., 132n
ambiguity, 26, 27-29, 32, 85-86
analysis, 5, 13
analytic account of philosophical
  statements, 27-29
analytic theory of philosophical disagreement, 14
anguish, 129-130
argument, 3-7, 21-25, 32-49, 52, 57-
  60, 64, 68-70, 76, 77, 81, 82, 93
  circular, 76-80
  defensive, 79
  destructive, 85
  inductive, 44
  interrogative, 85, 88
  question-begging, 63, 77, 80
  rhetorical, 55
argumentation, 5, 7, 56
argumentative context, 45
argumentum ad hominem, 3, 4, 65,
  69, 73-81, 87, 93-96, 104, 123-131
argumentum ad rem, 3, 76
argumentum ad seipsum, 79
Aristotle, 64, 65, 67-69, 86, 89, 90,
  112
assumptions, 25, 33, 34
audience, 44, 46, 52-56

B

behaviorism, 91
beliefs, 7-12, 16
Berkeley, 67-69, 90
bilateral aspect of philosophical disagreement, 19, 20
bilateral character of philosophical
  discussions, 51
bilateral power, 133, 134
Boolean algebra, 110, 118
Bradley, F. H., 90
British analysts, 86
  (*See also* "analysis")

C

Charge of Denying Presuppositions,
  90-92

Charge of Dogmatism, 86, 87, 92
Charge of Ineffectiveness, 89-90, 92
Charge of Self-Denial, 92
Charge of Self-Disqualification, 91,
  92, 104
Charge of *Tu Quoque*, 89, 92
Charge of Unintelligibility, 85
circularity, 98
  in definition, 99
  in proof, 99
classification of arguments, 82, 83
commitment, 12, 16-20, 52, 77, 124-
  132, 135
common-sense knowledge, 22, 134
communication, 83, 84
compromise, 19, 20, 52
conclusion, 58, 64, 65, 73, 76
conflict, 19
consistency, 114-115, 117-120
contingent relationship, 112, 113
controversy, 3, 11, 3, 14, 17-20, 35-
  37, 54, 130, 133, 136
copy theory of ideas, 101, 102
correction, 14, 15
Crahay, F., 116n
critical theory of philosophical disagreement, 17-19
criticism, 14, 15, 47-48, 64, 65
  destructive, 86, 88
  interrogative, 86, 88, 89

D

deduction, 34
defeat, 11, 12
definition, 28, 29
disagreement, 3, 7, 10-20, 52-56, 130
dialectic, 15
disputation, 10
dispute, 4

E

empiricism, 91
environment, 18
Eudoxus, 64, 65, 69, 90, 125, 126
evidence, 1-4, 7, 88, 119
existentialism, 2, 129
existentialists, 2
expression, 19